The Three Fat Pigs

Solimene's
PIZZA·PASTA·PANINI

# GROWING UP HAPA

## in Hawai'i

ĀHUALOA
FAMILY FARMS
Hawaii's
Oldest
Mac Nut Factory

# GROWING UP HAPA

*in Hawai'i*

Recipes and Stories *from*

CHEF IPPY AIONA

*photos by*

DUSTIN ACDAL

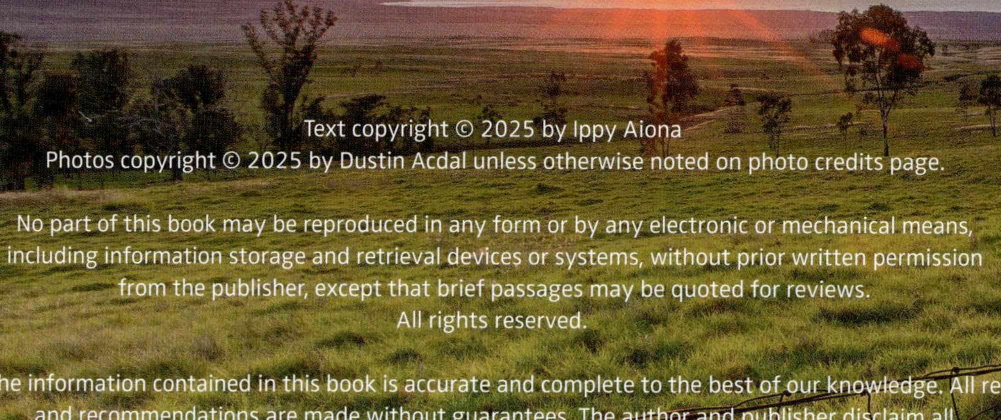



ISBN: 978-1-949307-76-4 // Library of Congress Control Number: 2025940117
Design by Jane Gillespie // First Printing, September 2025

Mutual Publishing, LLC
1215 Center Street, Suite 210 // Honolulu, Hawai'i 96816
Ph: (808) 732-1709 // Fax: (808) 734-4094
email: info@mutualpublishing.com // www.mutualpublishing.com
Printed in South Korea

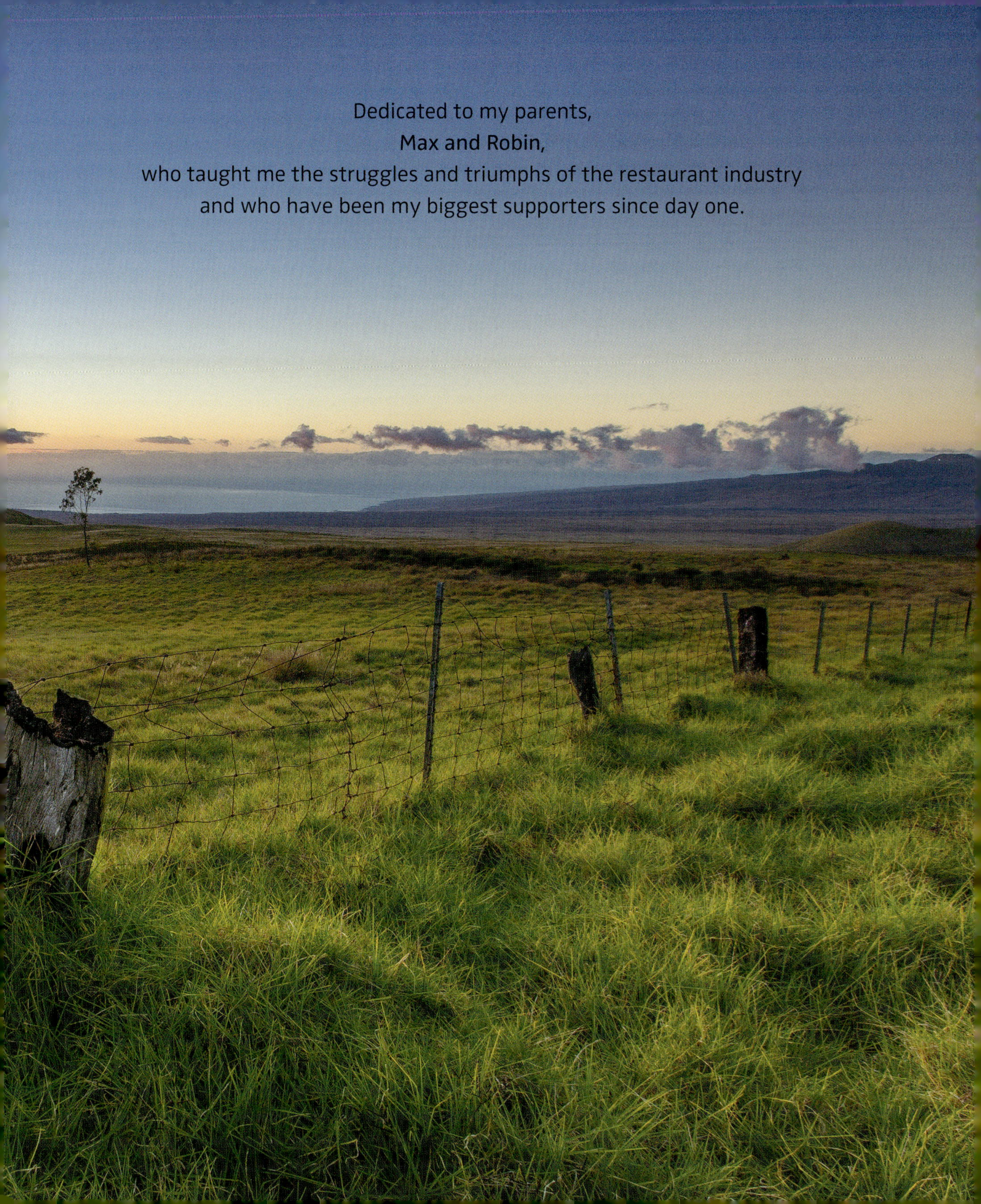

Dedicated to my parents,
**Max and Robin,**
who taught me the struggles and triumphs of the restaurant industry
and who have been my biggest supporters since day one.

# CONTENTS

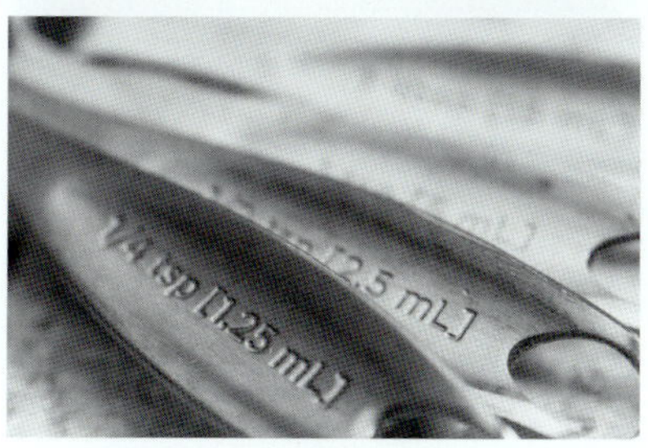
1/4 tsp [1.25 mL]
[2.5 mL]

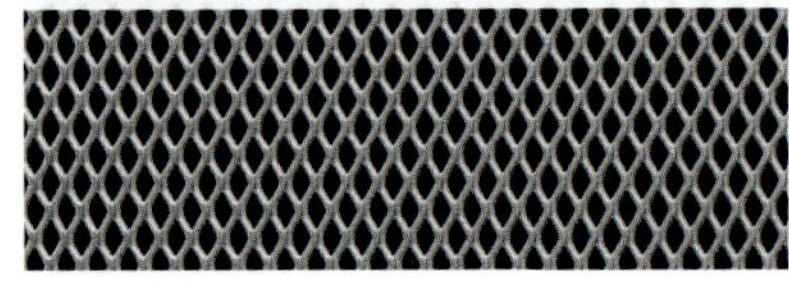

ALOHA
BARBECUE SAUCE

# ALOHA SHOYU

## *A Flavor Thread Through My Life*

Growing up in a Hawaiian plate lunch restaurant, certain ingredients become more than just kitchen staples—they become part of your everyday routine. Whether it was unloading giant Costco hauls or organizing deliveries, I got used to seeing the same items again and again: Calrose rice, Spam, and one of my personal favorites—soy sauce, or as we call it, shoyu. The brand we relied on the most was Aloha Shoyu.

At the restaurant, it was everywhere—five-gallon buckets in the back, gallon jugs in storage, and squeeze bottles lined up in the condiment bin for customers. It became so familiar that it embedded itself in my memory like a song stuck on repeat.

Aloha Shoyu is a family-run brand that was founded in 1946 by five local Japanese families in Kalihi. Over the years, their product line has grown to include teriyaki sauce, barbecue sauce, poke sauce, kalbi marinade, and of course, their signature shoyu. What sets Aloha Shoyu apart for me is its versatility—it's not overly salty, and its subtle, balanced flavor enhances marinades, sauces, and glazes without overpowering them.

My dad used Aloha Shoyu in his Hawaiian restaurant, and I've proudly carried on that tradition in my own plate lunch spot to this day. It's more than just an ingredient—it's a part of our story.

Beyond the kitchen, Aloha Shoyu has played a meaningful role in my professional journey. They've sponsored our show *Eating Our Roots,* and now they're part of this cookbook. Their commitment to family values and consistent quality says everything about who they are as a company.

From being a kid darting around their buckets in my parents' dry storage, to a chef instinctively reaching for their bottle during prep, and now a parent with it always on the table for my daughters—Aloha Shoyu has been with me every step of the way. It's more than a brand to us; it's part of our family, and I know it will continue to be part of our story for years to come.

# ABOUT THIS COOKBOOK

This cookbook isn't your typical collection of recipes divided by categories like "beef" or "sides." Instead, it's a deeply personal compilation of my life through food. Each chapter is a tribute to the different restaurants that I or my family have owned, and each one played a pivotal role in shaping my culinary journey. You might notice chapters dedicated to Italian cuisine, followed by those celebrating Hawaiian flavors and even a gastropub influence. It may seem like an unusual mix at first, but this is who I am.

Growing up hapa—with an Italian-American mother, a Hawaiian father, and a formal education from a classical French culinary school—has been a journey of blending vastly different cultural influences into one cohesive identity. It's not always easy to reconcile these diverse culinary worlds, especially when they are so distinct from one another. However, I've come to realize that they are all parts of me. Once I accepted that, my cooking and my perspective as a chef began to take shape, clear and true.

Each chapter in this book is like a window into my world, offering a taste of my mixed heritage and the diverse culinary traditions that have inspired me. These recipes are much more than just food; they are a reflection of who I am, where I've been, and the lessons I've learned along the way. The dishes you'll find here are deeply meaningful to me—they come from a place of passion, love, and the journey of embracing multiple cultural identities.

I want to take a moment to thank you in advance for sharing in these stories and recipes. They hold great significance in my life, and I'm honored to invite you into my world. I believe that life is a journey—one shaped by our childhood, our experiences, and the values we inherit. The person I am today is a direct reflection of the values instilled in me by my family and the restaurants I grew up in.

*Growing Up Hapa* is more than just a cookbook—it's an odyssey. It's a celebration of the flavors, traditions, and lessons that have defined my culinary career. I am truly grateful for the opportunity to share this part of my life with you, and I hope these recipes inspire you to embrace your own unique journey, whatever that may be.

# THE DEFINITION OF HAPA

The term hapa (hah-pah) carries a profound meaning, signifying someone of mixed racial ancestry, particularly those with Asian or Pacific Islander roots. In Hawai'i, the term often implies that Hawaiian is one of those ancestries. For example, I would be considered "hapa haole," a mix of Hawaiian and Caucasian heritage. Others might be "hapa Japanese," "hapa Chinese," or part of another blend, reflecting the beautiful diversity that defines modern Hawai'i.

Being hapa is a common experience in Hawai'i, as it's rare to find someone with entirely Hawaiian ancestry. For me, embracing my hapa heritage has been a journey of understanding the unique blend of cultures that make up my identity. My father is Hawaiian, Portuguese, and Chinese and my mother is Italian American. This combination technically makes me "hapa Italian," a label I wear with pride. What's fascinating is how similar Hawaiian and Italian cultures are—both place a strong emphasis on family, community, and food as the heart of their traditions.

My story is one of blending and honoring both cultures and finding harmony in their similarities while celebrating their unique differences. It's through this lens that I share my journey, inviting others to explore how food and family shape not only who we are, but also the legacy we pass on to the next generation.

Hapa is more than just a word. It is a lifestyle that we choose to embrace and use to mold who we are and where we come from.

# INTRODUCTION

I was born and raised in the small, peaceful town of Waimea on the Big Island of Hawai'i. Waimea is a place like no other. Surrounded by rolling hills and fertile volcanic soil, it's a town steeped in the rich culture of the paniolo—Hawaiian cowboys who helped shape this land. Growing up there, I was fortunate to live in a place that felt like a garden—everything from the lush, green landscapes to the fresh produce straight from the earth. As a child, though, like many kids, I didn't always appreciate the beauty surrounding me. You take things for granted when you see them every day, and I didn't fully grasp just how special my hometown was until I left. But as I grew older, I realized the protection and warmth this town offered me was one of the biggest gifts I could have received.

*Ippy on Moloka'i.*

Waimea is a town where life moves slowly, where people know each other by name, and where you never have to worry about locking your door. It is the kind of place where you can run out to the store for a gallon of milk, but somehow it takes you an hour because you bump into someone you know and "talk story" unfolds. It was the perfect town to grow up in—safe, full of heart, and brimming with a sense of community. I carry the spirit of Waimea with me everywhere I go. It's the foundation of who I am.

My dad is Native Hawaiian, born and raised in Hilo, and he is one of the hardest-working people I've ever known. He owned a local Hawaiian plate lunch restaurant called the Kamuela Deli, a place that felt more like a home than a business. I spent much of my early life there, watching my dad pour his heart and soul into his work. The menu was simple but full of love: lū'au stew, teriyaki chicken, loco moco, cheesy gravy burgers. Each dish was served with two scoops of rice, mac salad, and a side of cabbage under the meat, then packed in a styrofoam box with a drawing of a sunset and a palm tree printed on top.

The restaurant wasn't anything fancy, but it was the heart of our town—a place where locals gathered daily. After school, I'd walk to the deli with a friend, grab my meal, and join the regulars at the corner table. These old-timers would sit there, sipping coffee, puffing on cigarettes, and gossiping about anything and everything. I'd sit with them and do my homework, learning more from their stories than I ever did from a textbook. Their life experiences, their wisdom—it was a gift that I didn't even realize at the time. When the day ended, my dad would close up the shop, and we'd drive home together. The restaurant wasn't just a place to eat. It was where I learned what it meant to work hard, to be present, and to create something meaningful for your community.

On the flip side, my mom, originally from New York, carried a different kind of resilience. While she loved the beau-

ty of Hawai'i, she missed the flavors of her Italian roots—the pasta, the sauces, the warmth of her family's meals around the dinner table. Instead of feeling homesick, she channeled that longing into action and opened her own Italian restaurant. She was—and still is—a true entrepreneur. She's someone who believed in her dream so deeply that nothing could deter her. Watching her run Solimene's, a small Italian-American eatery with stucco walls painted in soft yellow with red trim, was nothing short of inspiring. The space was cozy, with arches leading into the kitchen, and the aroma of garlic, tomato sauce, and freshly baked bread filled the air. I grew up watching my mom juggle everything and work tirelessly to make her restaurant a success while still nurturing our family.

**The restaurant wasn't just a place to eat. It was where I learned what it meant to work hard, to be present, and to create something meaningful for your community.**

It was at Solimene's where I began to fall in love with the restaurant industry—where I learned what it meant to create an experience for people. The servers in black shirts would take orders and deliver bowls of baked pasta or pizzas. Genna, my future wife, would bake pastries in the back, and the restaurant would hum with the laughter and chatter of families enjoying their meals. I'll never forget how special it felt to be part of something that brought people together around a table.

When I graduated high school, I moved to San Francisco to attend the renowned Le Cordon Bleu, where I immersed myself in the art of French cuisine. But it wasn't just about learning how to cook; culinary school taught me about discipline, precision, and the beauty of technique. I met many

*Ippy and his wife, Genna, at The Three Fat Pigs.*

**I've found that this industry isn't just about cooking food for people—it's about creating a community, a family. The people who walk into our restaurants aren't just customers—they become part of our story.**

incredible chefs, including a beautiful Mexican chef who sat beside me on the first day of class. Although she only gave me a half-smile when I sat next to her, something about her caught my attention. Fast forward fifteen years and two children later, she's not only the love of my life, but also my lifelong sous chef and business partner.

Genna and I have built our lives and careers together, side by side. I always tell people that culinary school is what you make of it, and I made sure to give it everything I had. Graduating at the top of my class felt like just the beginning. My childhood in Hawai'i gave me a diverse understanding of food and culture, which helped me create dishes that fused different influences and techniques. I felt fortunate to have such a wide culinary foundation before entering school.

Since graduating, I've had incredible opportunities. I competed in shows like Next Food Network Star, Alex vs. America, BBQ Brawl, and even won Canada's International Iron Chef competition. The recognition I've received, including being named to Forbes "30 Under 30" list, is humbling, but what matters most to me is the impact I've had on the people around me.

At twenty-one, I opened my first restaurant, Solimene's Food Boutique and Espresso Bar, right next to my mom's place. Genna made the pastries, and I focused on coffee and

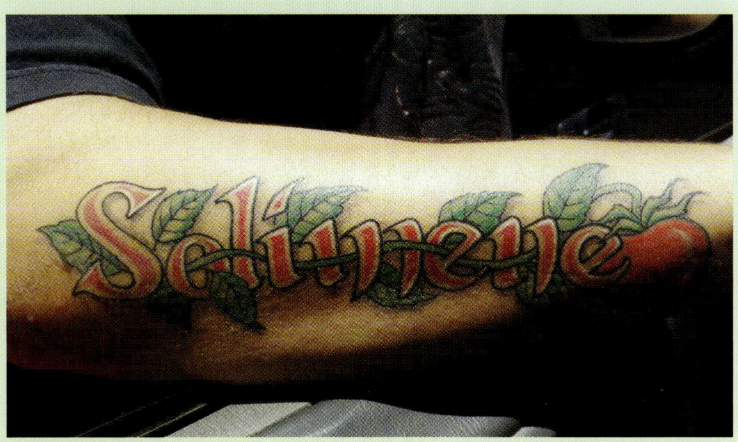

Grace and Poppy at Hāpuna Beach.

sandwiches, bringing a little bit of both of our worlds together. At twenty-three, I opened Ippy's Hawaiian BBQ in Waikoloa Resort—a tribute to my dad's plate lunch restaurant and the food that shaped my childhood. It wasn't a big place, but it had a giant mural of a hula dancer and the word "Aloha" written boldly across the wall—a simple yet meaningful representation of who I am.

My next venture, The Three Fat Pigs, was Hawai'i's first gastropub. It was a whimsical place, full of creativity and heart, and I learned so much about running a business and leading a team. The success of these restaurants has been built on more than just good food—it's about the connections we've made with our customers and the love we've poured into every dish.

Today, I'm back in Waimea, where I live with Genna and our two daughters, Grace and Poppy. It feels like life has come full circle. My daughters are growing up in the same town that shaped me, and I get to share the lessons I've learned with them. I've also opened my latest concept, The Dizzy Pita, a Mediterranean street food spot, and wrote my first cookbook, *The Easy Hawaiian Cookbook,* in 2022. My journey has led me to my proudest project yet, *Eating Our Roots,* an Emmy nominated food anthropology show that explores the ingredients, stories, and people that shape Hawaiian cuisine.

In every dish, every restaurant, every project, I've found that this industry isn't just about cooking food for people—it's about creating a community, a family. The people who walk into our restaurants aren't just customers—they become part of our story.

This cookbook, *Growing Up Hapa,* is more than just a collection of recipes. It's a reflection of my life—a life full of love, struggle, joy, and food that tells the story of who I am. It's my way of sharing the flavors of my upbringing and the lessons I've learned along the way. Each page, each recipe, is a piece of my heart.

# THE KAMUELA DELI

## *The Night It All Began*

I still remember that night with startling clarity—the night that changed the trajectory of my life forever. I was ten years old, sitting in the back of my parents' old Dodge caravan a few weeks out from Christmas. Rain drummed steadily on the roof, and cold, damp air seeped through the car windows as the heater struggled to keep up. Outside, the fog settled heavily over Waimea, thickening the quiet streets of our hometown on the Big Island of Hawai'i.

*Ippy wearing a haku lei.*

**To anyone else, the Kamuela Deli was just a tiny, unassuming hole-in-the-wall spot on the main road—a place people went to grab a quick plate lunch and move on. But to me, that place was magic.**

My dad was in the driver's seat, my mom beside him, and my big brother slouched next to me in the back, staring out at the rainy night. At that point, Dad managed a small plate lunch restaurant, a tiny spot in town known mostly to locals, while Mom handled its accounting. The restaurant was owned by a slim, reserved Chinese man named Albert Leong, who'd run the place for as long as I could remember. Money was always tight, and nights like this, crowded together in our old van, were about as close as we got to a family night out.

As I sat restlessly, tapping my fingers on the armrest, my parents turned toward us, their faces lit with expressions I didn't quite understand. Dad looked...excited, but there was something else there too—maybe a shadow of worry. Finally, he spoke, his voice wavering just a bit. "We have a surprise for you guys," he said, glancing over at my mom before going on. "It's big. And it means we won't be able to get a lot of Christmas gifts this year for you two... because Mom and I just got a loan to buy the deli."

The words settled slowly, and my brother and I stared, our mouths open, trying to wrap our minds around what this meant. To anyone else, the Kamuela Deli was just a tiny, unassuming hole-in-the-wall spot on the main road—a place people went to grab a quick plate lunch and move on. But to me, that place was magic. We only ate there on special occasions, basically whenever Dad could get a discount. In my mind, it was something like a world-renowned restaurant, the kind where I imagined famous chefs started their careers.

Dad grinned, his eyes catching ours in the rearview mirror, and asked, "Want to go inside and eat?"

Inside, the warmth of the deli kitchen enveloped us, the air thick with the smell of oil and shoyu and a hint of spice that had seeped into the walls over the years. My parents told us we could make whatever we wanted—anything. It felt like stepping into a dream. I still remember the sound of the deep fryer bubbling as I lowered a basket of scallops and shrimp into the hot oil, the sizzle and crackle filling my ears, smelling like the promise of something new. A simple dish—"Captain's Seafood Platter," they called it. But to me, it was more. It was a calling I hadn't known was waiting for me, unfolding right there, as if the smell of scallops and shrimp were promising me a future. Standing in that kitchen, for the first time in my life, I felt at home, comfortable amid the pots, pans, and kitchen equipment.

I felt a new weight—a pride and a responsibility, mixed with a thrill I'd never known. I glanced over at my parents, who were watching me, their faces full of love and a kind of nervous hope. I realize now that this was their dream, too, and that they'd put everything on the line for this chance, for us. As the smell of fry oil filled the air, I felt a warmth in my chest, something big and certain. I knew then, as surely as I knew the rain still fell outside, that I wanted to be part of this, to carry this moment forward. I wanted to be more than a kid with a dream—I wanted to make it real, for all of us. From that moment on, I knew exactly what I wanted to be.

Prep time: 1 hour
Cook time: 45 minutes

**SERVES 6**

# AUNTY VIVIAN'S CONE SUSHI

*Aunty Vivian is my great aunt, and she gave me this handwritten recipe. It's safe to say that at ninety-five she definitely knows what she is doing. I can still remember driving out to Hilo for New Year's Eve or a family pā'ina when I was young. Under the tarp tent, on the buffet line of food, there would always be Aunty Vivian's cone sushi centered between the smoke meat and pipikaula. Cone sushi, although not as fancy as other sushi, is delicious in its simplicity; with nowhere to hide, everything has to be good because there are so few ingredients. This simple dish is one of my favorites.*

- ½ cup rice vinegar
- 1½ cups white sugar, divided use
- 1 tablespoon salt plus 1 teaspoon
- 4 cups cooked white short grain rice
- 9 aburage, cut into half diagonally
- 12 cups water, divided use
- 2 teaspoons dashi granules
- 6 dried shrimp (optional)
- 3 teaspoons mirin
- 8 teaspoons Aloha Shoyu
- ¼ cup finely shredded carrot (about half a carrot)

*Aburage is Japanese fried bean curd and can be found in most Asian stores.*

**Make sushi rice:** In a small saucepan, combine the vinegar, ½ cup sugar, and 1 tablespoon salt. Heat over low heat until the sugar dissolves. Turn off heat and allow the liquid to come to room temperature.

In a large bowl, place the freshly cooked hot white rice. Gently fan the rice while slowly adding the vinegar mixture. Add the sauce a little at a time, fold the rice, and fan. Repeat until you use all the liquid or until you get your desired taste. Cover the sushi rice with a damp towel and set aside for at least 1 hour to cool.

**Make aburage:** In a medium pot, cover the aburage with 4 cups of water and simmer for about 3 minutes over medium-high heat to render the fat. Drain the aburage and transfer to a bowl and set aside.

In the same pot, combine the 8 cups of water, dashi, dried shrimp (if using), 1 cup sugar, 1 teaspoon salt, mirin and

Aloha Shoyu. Bring to a simmer over medium-high heat and add drained aburage. Cook for 30 minutes and strain; reserve liquid. Gently squeeze out any extra liquid from aburage. Set aside to cool.

Pour the reserved liquid into a small pot and over high heat, boil carrots for about 3 minutes until soft. Drain and fold carrots into the sushi rice.

**Assemble cone sushi:** Once cooled, on a clean work surface, open the cut side of the aburage to create a pouch, like a pita. Stuff the rice-carrot mixture into each aburage pocket. Repeat with the rest of the rice and aburage and serve cold.

*Uncle Dale, Uncle Roberto, Mom and Dad at the opening of The Three Fat Pigs.*

Prep time: 30 minutes
Cook time: 3 hours

**SERVES 8**

# PORTUGUESE BEAN SOUP

30 cups water
2 pounds smoked ham hock
1 yellow onion, blended in food processor
2 (15-ounce) cans tomato sauce
8 cups chicken broth
2 (10-ounce) Portuguese sausages, diced
3 stalks celery, diced
2 large carrots, diced
4 cups kidney beans
5 potatoes, diced
1 box tubetti
8 leaves kale, spine taken out and roughly chopped
1 tablespoon salt
1 teaspoon black pepper

*After sitting a while, the broth will get absorbed by the pasta, so feel free to add more chicken broth to make more soupy.*

*As with all my soups, this recipe comes from my mom's arsenal of amazing soups. Her Portuguese bean soup has impressed many a Portuguese customer and family members. It is a perfect hardy soup for cold nights. Portuguese sausage, or linguica, is a very popular sausage in Hawai'i with many locals making it in their backyard smokers and selling it on the side of the road or at farmers markets. Serve with some Portuguese sweet bread for a satisfying meal.*

**Make stock:** In a large pot, bring water, smoked ham hock, and onion to a simmer and cook uncovered for at least an hour until cooked down by half. Remove the ham hock, chop up all the meat, and add back to the broth.

**Start soup:** Add tomato sauce and cook down for another 30 minutes. Add chicken broth and Portuguese sausage and cook for another 30 minutes.

**Add aromatics:** Add celery and carrots and cook for another 20 minutes. Once carrots are a little soft, add kidney beans, potatoes, and tubetti, and cook on medium-low until pasta is fully cooked.

**Finish soup:** Add kale, salt, and pepper, and adjust seasoning to taste.

# MOM'S OXTAIL SOUP

**Prep time:** 20 minutes
**Cook time:** 3 hours

**SERVES 4**

- 14 dried shiitake mushrooms
- 3 cups water
- 4 pounds oxtail
- 1 gallon chicken or beef broth
- 3 thumb-size pieces of ginger
- 8 whole star anise
- 1 teaspoon whole black peppercorns
- 2 teaspoons salt
- 2 pieces chen pi (dried tangerine peels)
- 1 cup raw or lightly roasted peanuts, skin removed
- 1 mustard cabbage (kai choy), roughly chopped
- ½ cup chopped cilantro
- 8 scallion, green parts cut diagonally

*This oxtail soup is a cherished recipe passed down from my mom. The combination of dried shiitake mushrooms, star anise, tangerine peel, and peanuts creates a distinct, flavorful broth with incredible depth. While there are many variations of this dish, this Chinese-inspired version is the one that most closely resembles the version served here in the islands. Serve the soup with a variety of condiments in small bowls—like Aloha Shoyu, grated ginger, and sambal oelek—so everyone can customize their bowl. I also recommend making the soup a day in advance, as the flavors intensify overnight. Just be sure to keep the mustard cabbage separate and add it when you're ready to serve.*

**Prepare mushrooms:** In a large bowl, soak the mushrooms in 3 cups water to rehydrate. When soft, remove from water and slice mushrooms. Discard the hard stems and reserve the soaking liquid; set aside.

**Prep oxtail:** In a large pot, add the oxtail and cover with cold water. Bring to a boil over medium-high heat. When boiling, cook for 20 minutes then discard cooking water; rinse oxtail.

**Start soup:** Return the oxtail to a clean pot and add broth to cover. If there is not enough broth to fully cover the oxtail, add water. Add the ginger, star anise, peppercorns, salt, and chen pi. Simmer over medium heat partially covered for about 1 hour. Add the soaked mushrooms, reserved mushroom liquid, and peanuts. Continue to simmer, uncovered for 1½ hours until the oxtail is very tender. Skim the fat that rises to the top of the soup throughout the cooking process.

**Finish soup:** Add mustard cabbage and cook until just limp.

Serve the oxtail soup in bowls and garnish with cilantro and green scallions.

*Tangerine peel (chen pi) can be found in most Asian markets or stores online. Alternatively, you can make your own in advance and store in an airtight glass jar. Peel thin-skinned mandarins and scrape the white part off. String them together and hang in a sunny window with good airflow for a few weeks until perfectly dried. If you are in a hurry and don't have any chen pi you can substitute with strips of orange zest.*

Prep time: 20 minutes
Cook time: 45 minutes

**SERVES 4**

# TARO AND 'ULU CORN CHOWDER

1 large taro root, peeled and cut into 1 to 2-inch chunks (can use 3 russet potatoes instead)
1 tablespoon neutral oil
1 yellow onion, minced
1 celery stalk, minced
2 tablespoons butter
5 cloves garlic
2 tablespoons all-purpose flour
3 cups vegetable broth
1 cup heavy cream
1 cup milk
1 'ulu peeled and cut into 1 to 2-inch chunks
2 cups frozen corn (can use fresh)
3 dashes Tabasco
2 teaspoons Worcestershire sauce
Salt and pepper to taste

*I like to add 2 teaspoons of apple vinegar after the chowder is finished. It adds a bit of acidic balance and gives the chowder a beautiful shine.*

*This chowder was my dad's signature dish. On the Big Island, we have a valley called Waipi'o, renowned for its incredible taro and stunning waterfalls. The island is also home to the 'Ulu Co-op, a company that has made breadfruit ('ulu) more accessible across Hawai'i. I'll never forget a cooking competition I was in on Food Network, where the secret ingredient turned out to be 'ulu. To my surprise, it was the 'Ulu Co-op's product, and I couldn't have been prouder to see breadfruit take center stage on the national level.*

**Prepare taro:** In a pot, cover taro with water and bring to a boil. Cook until taro is fork tender. Drain and set aside.

**Cook aromatics:** In a separate large pot over medium heat, add oil and sauté the onion and celery for about 3 minutes, until translucent. Add the butter and garlic and cook until butter is melted and garlic is fragrant.

**Make roux:** Add flour and stir until the mixture thickens into a paste. Cook for 2 minutes, stirring continuously.

**Make chowder:** Add vegetable broth, cream, and milk and bring to a simmer. Add 'ulu and cook for about 20 to 30 minutes or until it is fork tender. Add cooked taro, corn, Tabasco, and Worcestershire and heat through. Season with salt and pepper.

Serve with some toasted bread.

# KOREAN BBQ CHICKEN

**Prep time:** 24 hours (if marinating overnight)
**Cook time:** 30 minutes

**SERVES 4**

- 1 cup water
- 1 cup white sugar
- 1 cup Aloha Shoyu
- 2 tablespoons minced garlic
- 1 tablespoon minced ginger
- 1 tablespoon toasted sesame seeds
- 2 teaspoons sesame oil
- 2 teaspoons sambal oelek
- 4 pounds boneless skinless chicken thighs, butterflied
- 3 tablespoons cornstarch
- 2 tablespoons water
- Chopped green onions

*If you don't have a grill, feel free to cook this in a sauté pan, the same process applies. You can also bake it in the oven on a sheet pan at 400°F for about 45 minutes or until it reaches an internal temperature of 165°F.*

*Korean BBQ chicken is extremely popular in Hawai'i. The Kamuela Deli had close to 200 different menu items and combinations, but this one was always one of the most popular. Growing up, my dad would take us to the beach and, armed with a ziplock bag full of marinated chicken, he would toss it onto the hibachi and let the hot coals worked their magic. I still take this whenever I take my family to the beach so my daughters can experience the same form of memories I have of spending time at the beach with my family.*

**Make sauce:** In a saucepan, bring water to a boil. Add sugar and stir until dissolved.

Turn off and add Aloha Shoyu, garlic, ginger, sesame seeds, sesame oil, and sambal oelek; cool to room temperature.

**Marinate chicken:** Place the chicken in a gallon ziplock bag. Add 1 cup of sauce to the bag, seal, and refrigerate overnight. Reserve any remaining sauce.

**Thicken sauce:** In a medium saucepan over medium-high heat, add the remaining sauce and bring to a simmer. Mix the cornstarch and water in a separate bowl and slowly add it to the simmering sauce until it thickens. You may not have to use all the cornstarch and water, as different brands make the exact amount hard to measure. Add the slurry until the sauce can easily coat the back of a spoon.

**Cook chicken:** On a hot grill, cook the chicken until it reaches an internal temperature of 165°F, brushing on the thick sauce until fully cooked.

Serve garnished with chopped green onion over hot rice or over a salad.

# CHICKEN LŪ‘AU

**Prep time:** 25 minutes
**Cook time:** 2 hours

**SERVES 6**

1 pound lū‘au leaves
5 cups water
1 tablespoon salt
3 tablespoons unsalted butter
½ yellow onion, blended in food processor
2 teaspoons minced ginger
2 cloves garlic, minced
1 pound chicken thighs, boneless and cubed in 1-inch cubes
1 cup chicken broth
1½ cups coconut milk
Salt to taste

*My dad always took great pride in his chicken lū‘au, swearing the secret was blending the onions in a food processor to ensure the flavors melded perfectly. This dish was a special at the Kamuela Deli and often didn't last the entire day, as it was always in high demand. I still have him make it from time to time for Ippy's Hawaiian BBQ. The difference between this and lū‘au stew is that chicken lū‘au is coconut milk based and lū‘au stew is broth based. Both are great but very different. A fun twist on squid lū‘au, this dish brings me so much comfort and nostalgia every time I enjoy it.*

**Cook lū‘au leaves:** Rinse lū‘au leaves; cut off stems and the thick veins, then cut into large pieces.

In a large pot over high heat, bring water and 1 tablespoon salt to a boil. Add lū‘au leaves and boil for at least 1 hour until lū‘au leaves are very soft. Make sure the lū‘au leaves are fully submerged, like boiling pasta. Remove and drain, squeezing out extra liquid.

**Make lū‘au:** In a large pot over medium-high heat, add butter and sauté the onions, ginger and garlic until fragrant, about 3 minutes. Add chicken and cook an additional 5 minutes. Add chicken broth, coconut milk, and cooked lū‘au leaves and simmer for another 45 minutes until chicken is fork tender. Enjoy.

Prep time: 15 minutes, plus marinating time
Cook time: 30 minutes

**SERVES 4**

# MOCHIKO CHICKEN WITH SPICY AIOLI

*Mochiko flour gets its name from the mochi flour (sweet rice flour) that is used to make it. Mochiko has a strong standing history when looking at the unique foods of Hawai'i. The sweet, crispy chicken has many different adaptations, though in this recipe, I dredge the chicken in the flour mixture to give it a crispy crunch. However, some people just put the chicken directly into the fryer straight out of the marinade to create a stickier texture. This beloved okazuya dish is something that is both unique and packed with flavor.*

- 2 pounds boneless skinless chicken, cut into 1 to 2-inch bite-size pieces
- 3 tablespoons cornstarch
- 2¼ cups mochiko flour, divided use
- ¼ cup white sugar
- 6 cloves garlic, minced
- 1 tablespoon minced fresh ginger
- 1 teaspoon salt
- ¼ cup Aloha Shoyu
- 1 teaspoon sambal oelek
- 2 large eggs
- Neutral oil for frying
- 1½ cups all-purpose flour
- ½ cup mayonnaise
- 2 tablespoons sriracha
- 1 teaspoon mirin

**Make marinade:** In a large bowl, combine the chicken, cornstarch, ¼ cup mochiko flour, sugar, garlic, ginger, salt, Aloha Shoyu, sambal oelek, and eggs; mix well. Cover and refrigerate for at least 3 hours, but preferably up to 24 hours for maximum flavor.

**Heat oil and dredge:** In a pot large enough to fry in, add about 2 inches of oil (enough to submerge the chicken) heat to 350°F.

In a separate bowl, mix all-purpose flour and remaining 2 cups mochiko flour.

After removing from fridge, mix the chicken well in the marinade as the cornstarch will have settled at the bottom. Then dredge each chicken piece one at a time in the flour mixture.

**Fry chicken:** Slowly add the dredged chicken to the oil and fry for about 8 minutes, until crispy and golden brown with an internal temperature of 165°F. Cook in batches as necessary. Transfer the fried chicken to a paper towel-lined plate to drain excess oil.

In a small bowl, whisk the mayonnaise, sriracha, and mirin together until well-mixed.

Serve by drizzling spicy aioli over the chicken. Or dip it!

Prep time: 30 minutes
Cook time: 1 hour

**SERVES 4**

- 10 dried shiitake mushrooms
- 3 cups water
- 1 tablespoon neutral oil
- 4 pounds boneless skinless chicken thighs, cut into bite-size pieces about 1 to 2 inches
- 3 gobo, cut diagonally about 1 to 2 inches
- 8 konbu, tied in knots
- 3 carrots, cut diagonally about 1 to 2 inches
- 3 aburage, sliced
- 1 cup sake
- 1 cup brown sugar
- 1 cup Aloha Shoyu
- 2 teaspoons salt
- 9 red potatoes, cut in 2-inch cubes

# CHICKEN NISHIME

*Chicken Nishime is a beloved Japanese dish that's especially popular in Hawai'i. You'll often find it in local okazuya (Japanese hot line restaurants), where it's always a crowd favorite. The dish strikes the perfect balance between sweet and salty, with each bite bursting with flavor. Of course, my dad makes the best nishime—though I may be a little biased! This recipe is his own, and it's a must-try. One of the daily specials at Kamuela Deli, it's a dish you definitely won't want to miss.*

**Hydrate mushrooms:** In a bowl, add dried shiitake mushrooms and water and allow to soak for an hour until soft. Cut off stems and cut mushrooms into slices. Reserve liquid.

**Cook chicken:** In a pot over medium-high heat, add oil and brown the chicken. Add water leftover from mushrooms and add sliced gobo. Lightly simmer the gobo until it is about halfway cooked (about 20 minutes).

**Finish:** Add konbu, carrots, aburage, mushrooms, sake, brown sugar, Aloha Shoyu, and salt; simmer for 15 minutes. Add potatoes and cook until potatoes and all vegetables are soft.

Serve over hot rice or on its own.

# NORI CHICKEN

**Prep time:** 24 hours (for marinating)
**Cook time:** 45 minutes

**SERVES 4**

5 (3-inch) pieces ginger, peeled
2 tablespoons water
½ cup Aloha Shoyu
¼ cup sugar
7 tablespoons cornstarch
3 large boneless skinless chicken thighs, cut in 2 x 3-inch large bite-size pieces
Toasted nori, cut into 2-inch wide strips
Neutral oil for frying

*Nori Chicken can be found in most okazuyas (Japanese hot line restaurants). Growing up at the Kamuela Deli we had a hotline on the side of the dining room. My parents, ever the entrepreneurs, would try many different things from okazuya to Chinese food. Whenever they would make okazuya food, this sweet, sticky, and delicious nori chicken was everyone's favorite, myself included. Although a little meticulous, this dish is totally worth all the work and looks as good as it tastes.*

**Make ginger water:** Grind the ginger in food processor with 2 tablespoons of water. Squeeze the ginger into a bowl to get all the ginger "water" out and discard ginger, saving the liquid.

**Mix marinade:** Add ginger liquid, Aloha Shoyu, sugar, and cornstarch; mix well. Add chicken to marinade and soak overnight.

**Cook chicken:** Bring a pot of oil to 350°F. Take each strip of chicken, wrap a piece of nori around the middle, and gently add to oil. Fry until golden brown and internal temperature of chicken is 165°F. Cook in batches until all the chicken is cooked.

Serve with a squeeze of lemon juice over rice or a fresh salad.

*« Steve Shropshire of Aloha Green on his ginger farm in Hilo.*

Prep time: 15 minutes
Cook time: 10 minutes

**SERVES 8**

# CORNED BEEF HASH

- 5 russet potatoes, peeled whole
- 3 (24-ounce) cans corned beef
- 3 eggs
- 1 teaspoon salt
- ½ teaspoon white pepper
- ½ cup sliced green onion (green part)
- 1 tablespoon neutral oil

*Masayo's corned beef hash became legendary in Waimea. Before she took the helm as chef at the Kamuela Deli, she ran a cozy diner in town called Masayo's, where her corned beef hash first gained its fame. With its crispy exterior and tender, flavorful interior, it's the perfect breakfast patty. Pair it with an over-easy egg, and you've got a dish that's satisfying any time of day—whether for breakfast, lunch, or dinner, it never disappoints.*

**Cook potatoes:** In a pot filled with water, add whole peeled potatoes to cold water. Cook until potato is soft enough for a fork to easily go through. Drain.

**Make patties:** Put potatoes in a bowl while they are still hot and add the corned beef, eggs, salt, and white pepper. Mix with a fork; mixture should be chunky. Gently mix in green onion.

**Cook patties:** In a sauté pan, add a little oil (about 1 tablespoon) and heat over medium-high. Make little patties out of the corned beef hash and carefully cook for about 3 minutes on each side until it is crispy and browned. Repeat until all hash is cooked. You can store the corned beef hash uncooked in the refrigerator for a few days.

*It is important to add the corned beef hash to HOT potatoes so the heat can melt the fat of the corned beef.*

# MASAYO'S BEEF STEW

**Prep time:** 30 minutes
**Cook time:** 2 hours

**SERVES 4**

- 2 pounds chuck roast, cut into 2-inch cubes
- 1 tablespoon neutral oil
- 12 cups water, divided use
- 2 teaspoons salt
- 1 large onion, cut in half and then each half cut into 6 pieces
- 3 celery stalks, cut into 2-inch pieces
- 2 cloves garlic, smashed
- 2 teaspoons tomato paste
- ⅓ cup ketchup
- 1 teaspoon freshly ground black pepper
- 2 jumbo carrots, peeled and cut into 2-inch chunks
- 2 large russet potatoes, peeled and cut into 1-inch cubes

*Masayo was truly special to me. She was the chef at the Kamuela Deli and the one who gifted me my very first knife—a Chinese cleaver. That moment marked the beginning of my journey to becoming a chef. Masayo's influence was so profound that I dedicated my first cookbook to her. Her beef stew may not be fancy, but it's flawless in its simplicity, and always delivers exactly what's needed—just like the incredible woman who created it.*

**Cook meat:** Rinse the meat and pat dry.

In a pot, add 1 tablespoon oil over medium-high heat and brown the meat. Once browned, add 11 cups of water and salt. Bring to a boil over medium-high heat and cook for 45 minutes. While simmering, skim off the fat and bubbles from the top.

**Start stock:** Once meat is soft and fork tender add onion, celery, and garlic and simmer for another 25 minutes.

**Make stew:** Add remaining 1 cup of water, the tomato paste, ketchup, and pepper; mix well. Add carrots and cook for another 20 to 40 minutes, or until the carrots start to get soft and fork tender. Finally, add the potatoes and cook until the potatoes are soft and easily pierced through with a knife, about 10 minutes.

*If you want more stew "gravy," add 3 more cups of water in the beginning.*

Prep time: 30 minutes
Cook time: 2 hours

SERVES 6

# DAD'S BEEF AND TARO LŪ'AU STEW

2 pounds lū'au leaves (young taro leaf), stem and vein cut out and leaf chopped into large strips
Water for boiling
1½ tablespoons salt, divided use
1 taro root, peeled and cut into 2-inch chunks
1 tablespoon canola oil
2 pounds beef brisket or short ribs, cut into 2-inch chunks
1 yellow onion, processed in food processor
2 teaspoons minced ginger
3 cloves garlic, minced
5 cups beef broth

*Lū'au leaf has a special enzyme (calcium oxalate) that when not cooked all the way will give you "itchy throat," as the old-timers call it, and it is extremely unpleasant. So, make sure it is cooked thoroughly.*

*I have made this recipe so many times in my life. I even featured it on my show,* Eating Our Roots, *with my dad as a special guest for our "Kalo" episode as it uses every part of the taro plant. I have also cooked it for many events, because it is always a crowd favorite. Simple yet bursting with flavor, it is the best kind of dish. Traditionally, it just has beef, but the addition of kalo adds some much-needed texture to the stew. My dad's trick is to process the onions well in a food processor because it helps disperse the flavors. Eat the stew with a big bowl of poi and be transported right back to the islands with one of my family's favorite meals.*

**Cook lū'au leaves:** Rinse lū'au leaves well. In a large pot, add water and 1 tablespoon of salt; bring to a boil. Use lots of water, as if you are cooking pasta. Cook lū'au leaves covered for at least 1 hour until soft but not breaking apart. Drain water and squeeze out any excess liquid from leaves.

**Cook taro:** In a pot with cold water, add taro and bring to a boil. Cook like you would potatoes until a fork easily penetrates the taro, for about 30 to 45 minutes. Cooking time can vary. Drain and set taro aside.

**Brown meat:** In a large pot over medium-high heat, add oil and brown beef. Once beef is browned, add onions, ginger, and garlic and sauté until nice and fragrant about 3 minutes. Add beef stock and ½ tablespoon of remaining salt; simmer covered until meat is fork-tender and soft.

**Finish stew:** Add cooked lū'au leaf and cooked taro. Simmer for another 30 minutes, taste, and adjust seasoning as desired.

Prep time: 20 minutes (or 24 hours if marinating)
Cook time: 45 minutes

SERVES 4

# SHOYU PORK

1 cup water
1 cup sugar
1 cup Aloha Shoyu
2 tablespoons minced garlic
1 tablespoon minced ginger
1 tablespoon toasted sesame seeds
1 tablespoon sesame oil
1 tablespoon sambal oelek
2 tablespoons neutral oil
2½ pounds pork shoulder, cut into 1 to 2-inch pieces
Green onion, sliced

*This simple dish is easy to make and was a crowd favorite at the restaurant. It embodies the perfect balance of sweet and salty that plate lunch food is known for, with a subtle kick of spice and the added depth of toasted sesame seeds to round out the flavors. Growing up, I'd often walk to my dad's restaurant after school, and one of my go-to snacks was a bowl of rice topped with this sauce. I have a feeling it's about to become one of your favorites, too.*

**Make sauce:** In a saucepan over high heat, bring the water to a boil. Add the sugar and stir until dissolved. Turn off heat and add Aloha Shoyu, garlic, ginger, sesame seeds, sesame oil, sambal oelek, and mix.

**Brown pork:** In a separate pot, add oil over medium-high heat and brown pork. Once browned, pour sauce over pork, reduce to a simmer, and cover. Cook for 30 to 40 minutes.

Remove the cover and cook for another 30 to 40 minutes or until the pork is fork tender. Garnish with sliced green onions and enjoy over rice.

*For the best flavor, make the sauce ahead of time and marinate the pork overnight.*

Prep time: 20 minutes
Cook time: 1½ hours

**SERVES 4**

# PORK AND WATERCRESS

- 2½ pounds of pork, cut in 1-inch pieces
- 1 teaspoon salt
- 1 tablespoon neutral oil
- 4 cloves garlic
- 1 tablespoon ginger
- 2½ cups chicken broth
- 2 teaspoons Worcestershire sauce
- 1 teaspoon Aloha Shoyu
- ¼ cup dried shrimp
- ½ teaspoon garlic powder
- ½ block firm tofu, cut into 1-inch cubes
- One bunch of watercress, bottom of stems cut off

*If you don't have dried shrimp, you can use 2 teaspoon of fish sauce.*

*Pork and watercress is a great opportunity to incorporate some greens into a dish. Watercress is ever-present in most grocery stores in Hawai'i. Growing up my mom always made this, and the Worcestershire is her little trick to add a bit of anchovy flavor into this aromatic dish.*

**Brown pork:** Season pork with salt. In a pan over medium-high, heat oil and brown pork. Add garlic and ginger and quickly sauté until fragrant. Add chicken broth, Worcestershire, Aloha Shoyu, dried shrimp, and garlic powder.

**Cook low and slow:** Lower to a simmer and cover for at least 1 hour until pork is fork tender. Uncover and add tofu and watercress. Cook for another 20 minutes. Enjoy over hot rice.

Prep time: 25 minutes
Cook time: 1 hour

SERVES 6

# PORK AND PEAS (GUISANTES)

- 4 tablespoons neutral oil
- ½ yellow onion, diced
- 8 cloves garlic, minced
- 4 pounds pork, cut into bite-size pieces
- 1 cinnamon stick
- 1 teaspoon ground cinnamon
- 2 tablespoons neutral oil
- ½ yellow bell pepper, cut into strips
- ½ red bell pepper, cut into strips
- ½ green bell pepper, cut into strips
- 1 teaspoon salt
- 2 teaspoons black pepper
- 1 tablespoon apple vinegar
- 6 bay leaves
- 1½ cups chicken broth (can substitute for water)
- 2 tablespoons fish sauce (patis)
- 2½ cups tomato sauce
- 2 cups frozen green peas
- 1 (7-ounce) jar pimientos (can leave out if you can't find)
- 1 tablespoon sugar

*This dish is a nostalgic favorite of mine—pork and peas. In Hawai'i, no Filipino celebration is complete without it; it's a true island staple. It's also one of my wife's all-time favorite Filipino dishes. The tanginess from the tomato sauce pairs beautifully with the savory depth of fish sauce, but what truly elevates this dish is the cinnamon. While not always included in traditional pork and peas recipes, it highlights the Spanish influence on Filipino cuisine and culture, adding a unique warmth and complexity to the flavors.*

**Sauté aromatics:** In a large pot, heat 2 tablespoons oil over medium-high heat. Add diced onion and sauté until translucent, about 3 minutes. Add minced garlic and cook until fragrant, about 1 minute.

**Brown pork:** Add pork, cinnamon stick, and ground cinnamon to the pot. Stir to combine and cook until pork releases its moisture and starts to brown, about 5 minutes. Cover and reduce heat to medium-low. Let cook for 15 minutes or until the liquid from the pork has evaporated.

Once the liquid has evaporated, uncover the pot, increase heat to medium, and let the pork brown for about 10 to 15 minutes, stirring occasionally.

**Cook bell peppers:** While the pork browns, heat 2 tablespoons oil in a separate pan over medium heat. Add bell peppers and sauté until softened, about 5 minutes. Set aside.

**Season meat:** Once the pork is browned, season with salt, pepper, and vinegar. Stir to combine and allow to cook for another 2 minutes for the vinegar to reduce.

**Simmer sauce:** Add bay leaves, chicken broth, fish sauce, and tomato sauce to the pot. Bring to a simmer and cook for 15 to 20 minutes, or until the sauce has reduced and thickened to your liking.

**Finish dish:** Stir in the peas, cooked bell peppers, and pimientos (if using). Cook for an additional 5 minutes. Taste and adjust seasoning with salt, pepper, and a pinch of sugar if you like a hint of sweetness to balance the acidity.

Serve hot over a bed of rice. Enjoy!

*The cinnamon really brings a unique warmth and depth, so don't skip it. It's key to capturing the flavor balance. Pimientos are optional and add a nice briny contrast to the dish, so I recommend using them if you have them on hand.*

Prep time: 25 minutes
Cook time: 20 minutes

**SERVES 4**

# CRAB RANGOON

5 ounces crabmeat
4 ounces cream cheese
1 teaspoon Worcestershire sauce
1 teaspoon Aloha Shoyu
½ teaspoon salt
½ teaspoon garlic powder
1 green onion, finely sliced
Neutral oil for frying
18 wonton wrappers

*Crab Rangoon has become a beloved dish at Chinese-American restaurants everywhere. It is originally believed to have come from the Polynesian-themed restaurant Trader Vics in San Francisco. I still remember making them at The Deli when they were far less common. At first, I thought the combination of cream cheese and crab seemed unusual, though it makes perfect sense considering how well cream cheese pairs with salmon. These crispy, light wontons are so irresistible that you'll have trouble stopping at just one. You can even prepare them ahead of time and freeze them before cooking. Don't be daunted by the steps—this labor of love is definitely worth every bite!*

**Make mixture:** In a bowl, mix crabmeat, cream cheese, Worcestershire, Aloha Shoyu, salt and garlic powder. Mix very well. Fold in the green onions.

**Fold wonton:** Lay out 3 wonton wrappers at a time. Place 2 teaspoons of filling in the center of each wonton and dab the edges with a little water. Fold the two corners together to make a triangle, wet two sides of the triangle and bring them together. Continue until all the filling is used.

**Fry wonton:** In a pot over medium high heat, add enough oil for frying and bring to 350°F. Drop the wontons into the hot oil for 3 minutes or until they are crispy and brown. Drain on a paper towel and enjoy hot with a sweet chili sauce or on their own.

*If crabmeat is too hard to find or too expensive, feel free to use imitation crab. It is used regularly for this dish and it still comes out delicious.*

# SHRIMP EGG FOO YOUNG

Prep time: 15 minutes
Cook time: 25 minutes

**SERVES 4**

½ head cabbage, shredded
½ carrot, shredded
1 yellow onion, julienned
2 tablespoons neutral oil, divided use
1 pound shrimp, deveined and cut into 1-inch chunks
1 teaspoon sesame oil
½ teaspoon white pepper
Pinch salt
Freshly ground black pepper
6 large eggs

*This is my version of the classic and extremely popular egg foo young. It is very close to what you would find at a good Chinese restaurant. My seafood and vegetable version is filled with cabbage, carrots, and onions and seasoned with toasted sesame oil. This is also a blank canvas dish, so feel free to use different vegetables or different proteins. This egg foo young just might end up replacing your favorite omelet or frittata.*

**Blanch vegetables:** Fill a large pot with salted water and bring to a boil. Blanch the cabbage, carrots, and onions. Don't cook too long as you want the vegetables to have a nice bite to them, so a quick 2-minute blanch will do. Pour into a colander and press down on the vegetables to squeeze out excess water; set vegetables aside.

**Cook shrimp:** In a sauté pan, heat 1 tablespoon oil on medium-high heat. Cook the shrimp until fully cooked, set aside.

**Combine batter:** In a large bowl, combine the cooled and drained vegetables, shrimp, sesame oil, white pepper, a pinch of salt, and black pepper. Mix to combine and taste to make sure it's flavorful. You can always add more salt and pepper if needed. Add eggs into the bowl and mix until well-combined.

**Cook dish:** In a nonstick pan over medium-high heat, add the remaining oil. Using a ladle, add the egg mixture into the pan to form a flat pancake shape. Cook on each side for about 5 minutes, until the egg is fully cooked.

Serve like you would your favorite omelet.

*Blanching the vegetables allows for a more even cook. If you like your vegetables a little more raw or crunchy, feel free to skip the blanching.*

Prep time: 20 minutes
Cook time: 10 minutes

**SERVES 2**

# SALT AND PEPPER SHRIMP

- 1½ pounds large shrimp, shell on and deveined
- 1 tablespoon white pepper
- 1 tablespoon ground black pepper
- 1½ teaspoons ground Szechuan peppercorns
- 2 tablespoons coarse sea salt or kosher salt
- ¼ cup cornstarch
- ¼ cup canola oil
- 1 tablespoon minced ginger
- 5 cloves garlic, minced
- 8 green onion, green and white parts, finely chopped

*If you can't find Szechuan peppercorns, you can omit. Just add a little more white pepper.*

*At Kamuela Deli, we had a special section of the hotline dedicated to my dad's Chinese dishes. One of the most popular was his Cantonese-style Salt and Pepper Shrimp. The addition of Szechuan peppercorns adds a distinctive numbing sensation that elevates the dish, making it both unforgettable and delicious. A beloved favorite at many Chinese restaurants, this simple yet flavorful recipe is easy to recreate at home—no intimidation required.*

**Prepare shrimp:** Rinse shrimp well and allow to dry on a plate with paper towels. In a large bowl, combine white pepper, black pepper, Szechuan peppers, salt, and cornstarch; mix together. Dredge shrimp in mixture.

**Cook shrimp:** Heat a pan over high heat and add oil. Once hot, quickly add ginger, garlic, and green onion for about 1 minute; remove and set aside. Add dredged shrimp to the pan and cook for about 5 minutes until fully cooked. Remove shrimp from oil with a slotted spoon and toss together with ginger, garlic, and green onions.

Serve over your favorite salad or as an appetizer by itself.

Prep time: 5 minutes, plus overnight chill
Cook time: 10 minutes

**MAKES 4 CUPS**

- ½ cup dried red chili flakes
- ¼ cup dried shallots or dried minced onions
- 3 tablespoons dried garlic
- 4 whole star anise
- 2 cardamom pods
- 3 tablespoons finely chopped fresh ginger
- 2 tablespoons white sugar
- 1 tablespoon salt
- 1 tablespoon Aloha Shoyu
- 1 teaspoon ground Szechuan peppercorns (optional)
- 10 cloves garlic thinly sliced
- 3½ cups neutral oil

*Use your favorite dried chili flakes, or you can get whole dried chilies and grind them in a food processor, using a colander to separate some of the seeds out. Dried garlic is available online.*

# GARLIC-CHILI OIL

*Chili crunch has become a culinary sensation, with countless chefs and companies creating their own unique versions. Some chefs even attempted to copyright the name, but were unsuccessful, as it's been around for so long. My version is one of my favorites—it's the perfect balance of spice, sweetness, and savory depth. This versatile condiment can be drizzled over anything: cold tofu for an appetizer, your favorite protein, as a salad dressing, or simply spooned over a bowl of hot rice. It's so delicious and adaptable that it had to make its way into this cookbook. I believe everyone should have a jar of it in their refrigerator, ready for those nights when you crave something simple yet flavorful. Stored in an airtight container, it'll last for up to two months in the fridge.*

**Combine aromatics:** In a large heatproof bowl, combine the chili flakes, shallots, fried garlic, star anise, cardamom pods, ginger, sugar, salt, Aloha Shoyu, and peppercorns (if using); set aside.

**Heat oil:** In a medium pan over medium-high heat, combine the garlic cloves and oil and slowly heat for about 5 minutes until garlic starts to turn golden brown.

**Temper ingredients:** Pour hot garlic oil over the chili mixture and mix until well-combined. Pour the chili crunch into a glass jar or bowl and let sit in the refrigerator overnight before serving. Store covered for up to 1 month in the refrigerator.

Prep time: 10 minutes plus 3 hours to set
Cook time: 20 minutes

**SERVES 4**

# BANANA AND CREAM COOKIE PARFAIT

- 1 (14-ounce) can sweetened condensed milk
- 1½ cups very cold water
- 1 (5.1-ounce) box vanilla instant pudding
- 3 cups heavy cream
- 1 (16-ounce) box gingersnap cookies, crushed (can substitute graham crackers, Oreos or Nilla wafers)
- 4 cups diagonally cut ripe bananas

*If you aren't eating these right away and want to assemble them ahead of time, squeeze a little lemon juice over the bananas after slicing to keep them from oxidizing and turning brown.*

*At the Kamuela Deli, we didn't have many desserts, but when we did, they were always simple and easy to make. Growing up, my grandparents ran a banana farm in Hilo, and every summer, my cousins and I would stay with them and help out. They grew a variety of bananas, from Williams bananas to cooking bananas, and apple bananas (my favorite). My grandma would always make this parfait and have them waiting in her refrigerator as a snack after cleaning and packing bananas all day at the farm—that's where my love for bananas truly began. This dish is a tribute to my childhood and my grandparents.*

**Make pudding:** In a medium bowl, mix the condensed milk and cold water until well combined. Add instant pudding and mix well. Cover and refrigerate for 3 hours until it sets and is cool.

In another bowl, whip the heavy whipping cream using a whisk until it is thick like whipped cream (feel free to use a mixer, or you can manually do it and get your workout in at the same time). Using a rubber spatula, gently fold the whipped cream into the pudding mixture, adding about a quarter at a time, fold from the outside in. Do not stir vigorously as you want this to be airy and light.

**Layer parfait:** In individual mason jars, or one large glass bowl, add a layer of the crushed gingersnap cookies. Add a layer of ripe bananas on top of the cookies. Top with a layer of pudding-cream mixture. Repeat the layering process until the jars are full.

# SOLIMENE'S

## A Family Legacy

Solimene's Italian restaurant was, and still is, a huge influence in my life. Even years after it was sold, it remains a part of who I am and is the foundation of my culinary point of view. Italian and Hawaiian culture may seem worlds apart, but their values—family, community, and tradition—are deeply intertwined. This book is my life in recipe form, and it would be incomplete if I didn't share the story of Solimene's.

**Pans clattered, timers beeped, tickets buzzed in, and the air filled with the aroma of tomatoes, garlic, and sizzling cheese. Everything that could go wrong did, but somehow, we pushed through. By the end of the night, we were exhausted but exhilarated.**

I was a junior in high school when I got *the* call. It was one of those defining moments, etched into my memory as if it happened yesterday. I was halfway up Laelae, a steep pu'u (hill) in Waimea, running for rugby training, when my phone buzzed. It was my dad and brother, their voices filled with excitement. "Macky and I just bought the Italian restaurant in town, for mom," my dad said, his words tumbling over each other. "We're gonna open Solimene's." My heart skipped a beat.

This wasn't just a restaurant—it was *our* restaurant, named after my mom's maiden name, Solimene. It felt like destiny. At the time, I knew I wanted to go to culinary school and become a chef, and this felt like the universe handing me a sign. The excitement coursed through me like a jolt of adrenaline. I sprinted the rest of the way up the hill, determined to get home and join them as they picked up the keys.

The name Solimene carried weight in our family. It represented more than food; it was heritage, pride, and a tribute to my grandpa. Back then, our little mountain town in the middle of the Pacific wasn't exactly a haven for authentic Italian cuisine. If you wanted quality ingredients, you had to really search for them. My mom wasn't deterred. She imported San Marzano tomatoes by the case, sourced whole wheels of Parmigiano-Reggiano, and tracked down bags of 00 flour. When she found out the only Parmesan available was the powdered kind in a plastic jug, she refused to settle. That spirit—of doing things the right way, no matter the effort—set the tone for everything we did.

The lead-up to opening was a flurry of activity. After wrestling practice, I'd drive to the restaurant to find my mom and her friend Patty painting the walls in shades of yellow and sienna, creating a warm, rustic stucco effect that transported you straight to the south of Italy. The restaurant felt alive even before it opened, with the scent of fresh paint mingling with the imported ingredients we unpacked

**It was my way of blending the flavors of my Hawaiian roots with the Italian techniques I was learning. That moment lit a fire in me—it was the first time I realized how deeply personal and creative food could be.**

from wooden crates. My baby brother, just a few months old, would often be fast asleep in one of those crates, nestled in his favorite blanket—a tiny reminder that this was truly a family affair from start to finish.

Opening night, however, was pure chaos—as first nights often are. The restaurant buzzed with energy with every table full, takeout orders galore, and the kitchen in a whirlwind. I was manning the pasta station while my other brother, only in his early twenties himself, manned the pizza oven. Orders poured in faster than we could handle. Pans clattered, timers beeped, tickets buzzed in, and the air filled with the aroma of tomatoes, garlic, and sizzling cheese. Everything that could go wrong did, but somehow, we pushed through. By the end of the night, we were exhausted but exhilarated.

When we got home, my mom had tears in her eyes. The physical toll of being on her feet all day was nothing compared to the emotional weight of realizing this was only the beginning. But in true mom fashion, she picked herself up and headed back the next morning at the crack of dawn to

start the marinara. With time and practice, the chaos found its rhythm, and Solimene's transformed into the heart of our town.

We became known for our New York-style pizzas, fresh pasta sauces, and perfectly pressed paninis. The restaurant was loud and lively, filled with the clatter of sauté pans, the rhythmic slap of pizza dough hitting the counter, and bursts of laughter from the dining room. It wasn't just a place to eat; it was a gathering spot where families celebrated birthdays, couples shared first dates, and regulars became extended family.

For me, it was more than a job. Solimene's was my playground, my proving ground, and the place where my culinary imagination began to take shape. I'll never forget creating my first special: *Kalua Pig Ravioli with a Brown Butter Charred Pineapple Sauce*. It was my way of blending the flavors of my Hawaiian roots with the Italian techniques I was learning. That moment lit a fire in me—it was the first time I realized how deeply personal and creative food could be.

Solimene's became my home base, my anchor. Whether I was coming home from high school or returning from culinary school, I always found my way back to its warm, familiar kitchen. The day it closed was bittersweet. By then, I had already opened my own restaurants, but the thought of saying goodbye was unbearable. I cleared my schedule, drove to Solimene's, and sat down for one last meal: a big bowl of baked ziti, stuffed shells, and a pizza. As I ate, memories flooded back—of the late nights, the laughter, the challenges, and the triumphs. A tear rolled down my cheek. It felt like losing a part of myself, like saying goodbye to a beloved family member who had shaped my life in ways I couldn't begin to measure.

Solimene's may no longer exist, but its legacy lives on—in me, in my family, in this cookbook, and in every dish I create. For that, I will always be grateful.

Prep time: 5 minutes
Cook time: 15 minutes

SERVES 2

# CRISPY SPICED CHICKPEAS

1 can chickpeas
Olive or canola oil for frying
3 cloves garlic, unpeeled
6 fresh sage leaves
Sea salt to taste
Cayenne pepper to taste

*This appetizer is the perfect pairing for a warm evening and a chilled glass of white wine. Known as "antipasto," this Sicilian-inspired dish is irresistibly addictive—like popcorn or potato chips—you won't be able to stop at just one!*

**Prep chickpeas:** Drain the chickpeas in a colander and rinse thoroughly with cold water. Transfer them to a paper towel and pat dry, ensuring they're completely dry.

**Fry chickpeas:** In a deep, heavy frying pan, pour oil to a depth of about 1 inch. Heat the oil to 375°F. Line a plate with paper towels to drain the fried ingredients after cooking. Once the oil is hot, add the garlic cloves and fry for about 1 minute, or until they begin to turn golden. Then, add the chickpeas and sage, frying for about 5 minutes, until the chickpeas are crisp and browned.

**Flavor chickpeas:** Using a slotted spoon, remove the chickpeas, garlic, and sage from the oil, and transfer them to the paper towel-lined plate to drain. While still hot, sprinkle the chickpeas with salt and cayenne pepper to taste.

*When frying the chickpeas, be careful because they can pop from the moisture. Cook in small batches, if easier.*

# ARTICHOKE AND SPINACH DIP

Prep time: 10 minutes
Cook time: 35 minutes

SERVES 4

- 1 can artichoke hearts (if you can try, to use non-marinated artichokes)
- ¼ cup sour cream
- ½ cup mayonnaise
- 8 ounces cream cheese
- 1 cup grated Parmesan
- 2 cloves garlic
- ½ cup frozen spinach, thawed, defrosted, and squeezed of excess liquid
- 1½ cups shredded mozzarella, divided use
- 3 dashes Tabasco
- 2 teaspoons Worcestershire sauce

*For an extra little kick you can add crispy bits of bacon into the dish.*

*This is a pretty common dish at many Italian restaurants and for good reason—it is creamy, tangy, and delicious. At Solimene's it was one of our more popular appetizers. I love this dish because it can be made ahead of time and stored in the fridge (or even the freezer) for a couple of days until you need it. Try this simple dish for a quick and easy appetizer.*

Preheat oven to 375°F.

**Mix ingredients:** In a food processor, add everything except for 1 cup of mozzarella. Blend together until everything is well mixed.

**Bake:** Spread artichoke dip into a baking dish (8 x 8-inch will work, but two smaller pans could work, too). Bake covered for about 20 minutes until the dip is hot. Uncover and sprinkle remaining shredded mozzarella evenly on top and return to the oven, cooking until it is melted and golden brown in spots.

Serve with toasted bread or tortilla chips.

Prep time: 20 minutes
Cook time: 45 minutes

SERVES 4

# ROASTED TOMATO GORGONZOLA SOUP

- 8 Roma tomatoes, quartered
- 2 tablespoons olive oil, divided use
- 1 teaspoon salt
- ½ teaspoon dried oregano
- 1 onion, minced
- 8 cloves garlic, minced
- 1 (1-pound, 12-ounce) can peeled tomatoes (preferably San Marzano)
- 4 cups chicken broth
- ½ cup Gorgonzola
- 5 basil leaves
- 1 cup cream
- 2 teaspoons salt

*In our house and restaurant, my mom had her own nickname: "The soup goddess." It was a very fitting name as her soups were the type that not only satisfied your stomach but also your soul. This particular soup is my two-year-old daughter's favorite soup. The blue cheese and cream are the perfect balance to the acidic tomatoes and this is THE BEST soup to eat with a grilled cheese sandwich. The soup goddess strikes again!*

---

**Cook tomatoes:** Preheat oven to 400°F. Add quartered Roma tomatoes to a sheet pan or roasting pan. Toss the tomatoes with 1 tablespoon olive oil, salt, and oregano. Roast for about 45 minutes until the tomatoes start to caramelize.

**Add aromatics:** In a pot on medium-high heat, add 1 tablespoon olive oil and minced onion and cook for about 3 minutes until onions become translucent. Add garlic and cook for another 2 minutes; do not burn garlic.

**Make soup:** Add canned whole tomatoes one at a time, crushing them in your hand while adding them. Allow to simmer for about 10 minutes. Add chicken broth, Gorgonzola, and basil leaves and bring up to a simmer.

**Blend soup:** Using an immersion blender, blend soup until it is smooth. If you don't have an immersion blender you can add the soup in batches to a blender, but be careful and vent the top so it doesn't blow up all over your kitchen. Once everything is blended smooth, add the cream and salt. Season to taste.

Serve with some delicious bread.

Prep time: 45 minutes
Cook time: 35 minutes

**SERVES 4**

# ROASTED RED PEPPER SOUP

- 5 roasted red peppers, peeled and seeded
- 2 tablespoons olive oil
- 1 yellow onion, diced
- 1 carrot, diced
- 6 cloves of garlic, minced
- 1 tablespoon tomato paste
- 6 cups chicken broth (can use vegetable broth also)
- 6 basil leaves, chopped into strips
- 2 cups cream
- 2 tablespoons unsalted butter
- ¼ cup grated Romano cheese (can use Parmesan)
- 1 teaspoon salt

*This soup is divine, coming straight from the culinary expertise of my mom, the soup goddess! It's a dish that earns its place as a winner in any kitchen. I typically opt for canned roasted red peppers for convenience, but if you have the time, I highly recommend fire roasting your own red bell peppers. The process of peeling and deseeding them adds an incredible depth of flavor that elevates the soup to new heights. To add a twist, I love to top the soup with toasted sunflower seeds, which provide a satisfying crunch and a nice contrast to the creamy texture. With every spoonful, you can expect a wave of creamy deliciousness that will surely warm your heart and soul. Get ready to savor this delicious creation!*

---

**Roast peppers:** If you are using raw red bell peppers, set your oven to 450°F and cut the peppers in half (remove the stem and seeds). Place on a sheet pan lined with foil cut side down and roast for 15 to 20 minutes or until the skins are very dark and have collapsed. Remove from oven and allow to cool so you can handle them. Peel off skin (they should slip off easily).

**Make soup:** Add olive oil to a pot over medium-high heat. Cook onions and carrots for about 5 to 8 minutes until the carrots start to get soft. Add garlic and tomato paste and cook for another 3 minutes allowing the tomato paste to caramelize a little. Stir in roasted peppers and cook for another 5 minutes. Add chicken broth and basil and turn down to a simmer. Cook for about 25 minutes until the carrots are very soft.

**Blend soup:** Using an immersion blender (you can use a regular blender, just do in batches and make sure to vent the top so it doesn't blow on you). Blend everything until smooth. Stir in cream, butter, and cheese and allow to simmer together for just a few minutes. Finish with salt and adjust to taste. I serve this soup with a few sunflower seeds and freshly cracked pepper.

Prep time: 30 minutes
Cook time: 1 hour

**SERVES 6**

# MINESTRONE SOUP

2 tablespoons olive oil
½ yellow onion, minced
2 carrots, diced
1 leek, white part, sliced thin
3 stalks celery, diced
6 cloves garlic, minced
5 basil leaves, chiffonade
½ pound peeled canned tomato (or three regular tomatoes cut into quarters)
8 cups chicken broth
3 potatoes, diced
1½ cups dried tubetti pasta
1 zucchini, diced
2 tablespoons minced parsley
1 teaspoon minced fresh thyme
Salt and pepper to taste

*Feel free to add whatever vegetables or beans you want to this dish, just make sure to cook at different times so your vegetables don't get mushy. A nice bite to the vegetables really makes this dish good.*

*This soup reminds me of cold Waimea mountain nights after football practice, because it is something my mom would always make us. She would make me cut the vegetables though, because they all have to be cut small and uniformly, which is probably the most time-consuming part. This comforting vegetable soup is a true one pot comfort dish that will warm up the family on cold nights.*

**Cook aromatics:** In a pot over medium-high heat, add olive oil, onions, carrots, leeks, and celery; sauté for 5 minutes. Add garlic and basil and cook quickly until you can smell the garlic.

**Add tomatoes:** Crush the canned tomatoes with your hands and pour into the pot. Cook for 10 more minutes.

**Finish soup:** Pour in chicken broth and cook until carrots and celery are tender. Add potatoes and bring back to a simmer. Pour in tubetti, zucchini, parsley, and thyme, and simmer until pasta is fully cooked. Remove from heat and season to taste.

Prep time: 20 minutes
Cook time: 40 minutes

**SERVES 4**

# PASTA E FAGIOLI SOUP

1 tablespoon olive oil
¼ cup pancetta, chopped into small pieces
3 tablespoons olive oil
1 yellow onion, finely chopped
1 carrot, diced
1 celery stalk, diced
2 cloves garlic, minced
½ pound San Marzano tomatoes, hand-crushed
8 cups chicken broth
2 cups tubetti pasta
½ cup kidney beans, drained and rinsed
½ cup cannellini beans
¼ cup grated Romano cheese
Salt and pepper to taste

*Pasta e fagioli, or "pasta fazool" as my mom and most New Yorkers call it, is a delicious bean and pasta soup. A regular staple on the soup of the day menu at Solimene's, this soup is packed with tons of flavor. My mom's secret is to add a cheese rind to the soup while its cooking and then remove it once it's done. This adds a ton of depth to the soup and also helps use up the extra cheese rinds that we have lying around the restaurant. I love pasta fazool and so do my daughters. This is a go to soup in my household.*

**Cook pancetta:** Bring a pot to medium high heat and add olive oil. Cook the pancetta, constantly stirring until nice and crispy.

**Add aromatics:** Add 3 tablespoons olive oil. Add onions, carrots, and celery and cook until the onions are golden, about 8 minutes. Add garlic and quickly cook taking care not to burn the garlic.

**Make soup:** Add tomatoes and broth. Reduce heat and simmer until the vegetables are tender, about 15 minutes. Raise the heat back to medium and add pasta and beans. Cook until pasta is al dente. Finish by stirring in Romano cheese. Season with salt and pepper to taste.

Prep time: 20 minutes
Cook time: 45 minutes

**SERVES 4**

# PANCETTA AND CARAMELIZED ONION SOUP

1 tablespoon olive oil
1½ cups chopped pancetta
2 tablespoons butter
2 teaspoons sugar
3 large yellow onions sliced (julienned)
Pinch of red pepper flakes
¼ cup red wine
1 (1-pound, 12-ounce) can peeled tomatoes (preferably San Marzano)
6 cups chicken broth
1 teaspoon salt
½ cup grated Romano cheese (can use Parmesan)
5 basil leaves, sliced thin (chiffonade)
Salt and pepper to taste
Minced parsley for garnish

*If you can't find pancetta, feel free to use a cured bacon. Just don't use maple or any flavored bacon.*

*When I returned home from culinary school, I jumped right back into the kitchen at Solimene's, working the line where it all began. Like most fresh culinary graduates, my head was buzzing with ideas—some ambitious, some chaotic, and only a handful truly worth exploring. But this dish? This one was special. Drawing inspiration from my training at a French culinary school, I wanted to reimagine a classic French onion soup with an Italian twist. The result was a dish that blended tradition and creativity seamlessly. Sweet, caramelized onions formed the heart of the dish, their richness balanced by the bright acidity of tomatoes. The addition of pancetta brought a luxurious, smoky depth, tying everything together in a perfect harmony of flavors. Each bite was bold yet balanced—a comforting bowl that celebrated both my culinary roots and my creative aspirations.*

**Cook pancetta:** Bring a pot to medium high heat and add olive oil. Cook the pancetta, constantly stirring until nice and crispy.

**Add aromatics:** Once pancetta looks crispy, lower heat to medium-low. Add the butter, sugar, sliced onions, and red pepper flakes. This step is going to take a little time and patience to slowly cook the onions until they are a nice golden brown.

**Add wine:** When onions are caramelized, add wine and cook down by half.

**Cook tomatoes:** Add the can of tomatoes, hand-crushing each one when putting them into the pot. Do not add the tomatoes without crushing them first. Cook down for about 10 minutes. My mom says to cook them until you cook out the "can" taste.

**Finish soup:** Add chicken broth, salt, cheese, and basil and simmer for about 5 minutes. Taste and season with salt and pepper, if desired. Garnish with minced parsley.

Prep time: 30 minutes
Cook time: 40 minutes

SERVES 4

# GRILLED SUMMER VEGETABLE AND GOAT CHEESE PENNE PASTA

- 10 cloves garlic
- 8 basil leaves
- ¼ cup olive oil
- 2 cups penne pasta
- 1 zucchini, sliced into rounds
- 1 Japanese eggplant, cut into rounds
- 6 asparagus, bottoms cut off
- 1 tablespoon olive oil
- ½ red onion, sliced julienne
- 1 handful (about 15) cherry tomatoes, halved
- Pinch red pepper flakes
- ¼ cup white wine
- 4 ounces or 5 tablespoons of goat cheese
- ¼ cup pasta water
- 5 basil leaves, chiffonade (sliced thin)

*Make a little extra garlic sauce, put it into a jar, and store in your refrigerator for up to a week. Use it for garlic bread or to add some flavor to anything you are making.*

*On Hawai'i's Big Island, we're fortunate to have some of the finest goat cheese you'll find anywhere, and it's the key ingredient that makes this dish shine. Creamy with just the right hint of acidity, the goat cheese is undeniably the star, bringing richness and balance to every bite. While we do have seasons here, they're subtler than most places, and the island's year-round bounty allows for incredible flexibility. Feel free to use whatever grilled vegetables you have on hand—this dish celebrates freshness and adaptability, making it as versatile as the island itself.*

---

**Make garlic sauce:** In a food processor, add garlic, basil, and olive oil and blend until it is the consistency of a pesto. If you don't have a food processor mince everything fine and mix in a bowl.

**Boil pasta:** In a large pot on high, boil pasta for 15 minutes or until the texture you desire. Make sure the water is heavily seasoned with salt. Reserve ¼ cup of the pasta water. Rinse pasta and set aside.

**Cook vegetables:** Preheat grill to at least 400°F. In a mixing bowl, add zucchini, eggplant, asparagus, and add 1 tablespoon of the garlic sauce; toss together. Grill vegetables and set aside.

**Make sauce:** In a pan large enough to fit all the pasta, heat 1 tablespoon of oil to medium high and sauté red onions for about 5 minutes to cook down and caramelize a little. Add cherry tomatoes and red pepper flakes and continue to sauté for about 3 minutes. Add 2 tablespoons of the remaining garlic sauce and quickly cook for about 2 minutes, making sure to not burn the garlic. Pour in white wine and cook down for another 2 minutes. Add goat cheese and pasta water one tablespoon at a time until a sauce forms (you don't have to use all the pasta water).

**Finish dish:** Toss pasta into sauce and add grilled vegetables. Mix all together to coat pasta and vegetables in sauce. Top with basil.

Prep time: 25 minutes
Cook time: 45 minutes

**SERVES 4**

# SPAGHETTI ALLA PUTTANESCA

- 1 pack spaghetti
- 2 tablespoons olive oil
- 8 canned anchovy fillets
- 1 yellow onion, diced
- 8 cloves garlic, minced
- 1½ teaspoons red pepper flakes
- ½ cup white wine
- 3 pounds canned whole peeled tomatoes (preferably San Marzano), hand-crushed
- 5 basil leaves, cut into very thin strips (chiffonade)
- 2 teaspoons salt
- ½ cup capers, rinsed and drained
- 1 cup pitted and sliced kalamata olives
- 1 cup sliced black olives
- 2 tablespoons minced Italian flat leaf parsley

*If you like spice, feel free to add more pepper flakes.*

*When I was getting my arm sleeve tattoo, I knew I wanted something that I not only loved in the moment but would continue to love forever. What I chose was puttanesca. The entire recipe, from the anchovies to the capers, is tattooed on my arm as a testament to my deep love for this dish. The name "puttanesca" translates to "in the style of the lady of the night," and it was created in Italy with the intention of being a simple, go-to sauce made from ingredients you always have on hand. The anchovies melt into the sauce, infusing it with a rich, briny flavor, while the olives add saltiness that complements the sweetness of the San Marzano tomatoes perfectly. Give this sauce a try, and you too might get it tattooed on your arm.*

**Boil pasta:** In a large pot of salted water over high heat, cook the spaghetti until it reaches your desired texture. Drain and set aside.

**Start sauce:** In a separate pot, heat 2 tablespoons of olive oil over medium heat. Add the anchovy fillets and cook until they break down and melt into the oil.

**Cook aromatics:** Add the onion and cook for 2 minutes, or until the onions become translucent. Stir in the garlic and red pepper flakes, cooking just until the garlic becomes fragrant.

**Finish sauce:** Pour in the white wine and let it cook down for about 5 minutes. Add the crushed tomatoes, basil, salt, capers, and both olives. Simmer lightly for 30 minutes.

Top with fresh parsley and serve over the cooked spaghetti.

# SPAGHETTI CARBONARA

Prep time: 15 minutes
Cook time: 25 minutes

**SERVES 4**

- ½ pound spaghetti
- 1 tablespoon olive oil
- 1 cup diced pancetta (you can substitute bacon, but not maple flavor)
- Pinch red pepper flakes
- 10 cloves garlic, minced
- ¾ cup white wine
- 2 eggs, beaten
- ¼ cup Parmesan cheese
- Salt and pepper to taste
- 1 tablespoon chopped parsley

*If I had one last dish to eat, this would be it. I first learned how to cook this dish while on a trip to Europe by a large Italian chef, and he made it clear that most people make this recipe wrong. It's all about simplicity when it comes to carbonara. I tell everyone it is the best "bacon and eggs" you will ever eat. The egg becomes the creamy sauce of this dish, so please be careful to not scramble the egg. No cream, no mushrooms, and no peas; this is the way carbonara should be eaten!*

**Cook pasta:** In a large pot on high, bring water to boil and cook pasta to desired texture. Make sure water is heavily seasoned with salt. Drain, rinse and set aside.

**Cook pancetta and garlic:** Add 1 tablespoon oil to a pan on medium-high heat and cook pancetta until crispy. Add red pepper flakes and garlic and cook for only another minute, making sure garlic doesn't burn.

**Make sauce:** Add white wine and cook down by half. Add pasta and cook until the wine is absorbed and pasta is hot. Turn off heat and remove from the hot burner. Slowly add the eggs while also stirring the pasta, this part is very important as you don't want the egg to scramble. It should create a beautiful creamy sauce. Add the cheese and mix together. Season with salt and pepper to taste and finish with chopped parsley.

*To prevent the eggs from scrambling, you can add about 1 tablespoon of hot pasta water to the eggs to temper them before adding to the sauce.*

# PENNE ALLA VODKA

**Prep time:** 20 minutes
**Cook time:** 45 minutes

**SERVES 4**

1 pound penne
1 tablespoon olive oil
¼ cup pancetta, chopped (optional)
2 cloves garlic, minced
4 tablespoons unsalted butter
1 (1-pound) can whole peeled tomatoes, hand-crushed
Pinch red pepper flakes
Salt to taste
¼ cup vodka
½ cup heavy cream
½ cup grated Parmesan cheese

*This dish is a beloved New York Italian American staple. Solimene's vodka sauce, one of the restaurant's signature sauces, makes this my little brother's all-time favorite pasta. Every time he comes home from college, it's the first thing he asks my mom to make. Creamy, tangy, and perfectly balanced, this sauce is an ideal choice for a quick, satisfying family dinner that never fails to impress.*

**Cook pasta:** In a large pot of heavily salted water over high heat, boil pasta until desired texture is reached. Reserve about a cup of the pasta water and set aside.

**Cook sauce:** In a large pan over medium-high heat, add olive oil and cook pancetta until crispy. Add garlic and cook for another 2 minutes; don't burn the garlic. Add the butter and let it melt. Stir in tomatoes, red pepper flakes, and salt to taste. Bring the sauce to a simmer and cook for 5 minutes. Add vodka and heavy cream to sauce and cook for another 20 minutes. At this point you can add some of the pasta water if your sauce is too thick (you don't have to use all the pasta water).

**Finish sauce:** Toss in pasta and remove from heat. Add grated cheese and toss well with pasta and sauce.

*Brent Sasaki of Cal-Kona Produce in Kealakekua on the Big Island.*

Prep time: 20 minutes
Cook time: 30 minutes

SERVES 4

# BUCATINI ALLA AMATRICIANA

1 pound bucatini or spaghetti
2 tablespoons olive oil
¼ pound guanciale or pancetta, chopped
1 small yellow onion, chopped
2 cloves garlic, minced
Pinch red pepper flakes
2½ cups strained tomato sauce
Salt to taste
⅓ cup grated Romano cheese

*Amatriciana hails from a small town near Rome called Amatrice, and trust me, they know how to make a phenomenal pasta sauce! The richness and saltiness of the guanciale truly steal the show in this dish. Bucatini, a pasta similar to spaghetti but with a hole running through the center, is the perfect choice. The hollow shape allows the sauce to cling to every bite, ensuring no mouthful is without flavor. At Solimene's, we often featured this dish as a special, swapping the traditional strained tomato sauce for our signature house marinara. I still remember making this dish, adding anchovies and eating it over rice (don't tell my mom). Try making this sauce at home for a comforting, delicious meal that never disappoints.*

**Cook pasta:** In a large pot of heavily salted water over high heat, bring water to a boil and cook pasta to desired texture, reserve 4 ounces of pasta water; drain and set aside.

**Cook sauce:** In a pan over medium high heat, add olive oil and cook the guanciale until browned, for about 10 minutes. Add onions and cook until translucent about 5 minutes. Add garlic and red pepper flakes and cook another 2 minutes. Pour in tomato sauce and a pinch of salt; simmer for about 15 minutes until sauce is thickened.

**Finish sauce:** Sprinkle grated Romano into the sauce and toss well, you can loosen sauce with pasta water if desired. Season to taste and toss in pasta.

*Guanciale is cured pork cheek with salt and pepper, but if you can't find this amazing ingredient, pancetta (cured pork belly) will work just as well.*

**Prep time:** 10 minutes
**Cook time:** 45 minutes

**SERVES 4**

# BACON AND BLUE CHEESE MACARONI GRATIN

½ box macaroni (or tubetti)
1 tablespoon neutral oil
8 strips bacon, cut into ½-inch pieces
½ yellow onion, diced
3 tablespoons butter
5 tablespoons flour
4 cups half-and-half
½ cup blue cheese
¼ cup Parmesan or Romano
½ teaspoon salt
Pinch black pepper
Pinch white pepper
¼ cup of shredded mozzarella

*My mom always had a saying at Solimene's: "If something is good, add fat and it will become great." By that standard, this sauce is fantastic. Rich, creamy blue cheese flavors are complemented by crispy bits of bacon, making this macaroni gratin a foolproof hit. If you're a blue cheese lover, you absolutely have to try this dish—trust me, you're going to love it!*

---

**Cook pasta:** Boil the pasta in salted water until it reaches your desired texture, then drain and set aside.

**Crisp bacon:** In a large pan, heat 1 tablespoon oil over medium-high heat. Add chopped bacon and cook until crispy; leave the rendered fat in the pan.

**Sauté onions:** In the same pan, add the finely diced onion to the bacon and sauté until the onions become soft and translucent, about 4 minutes.

**Make the roux:** Add butter to the pan with the bacon and onions. Allow the butter to melt and combine with the rendered fat. Once melted, whisk in the flour and cook for about 2 minutes, stirring constantly.

**Make sauce:** Gradually pour in the half-and-half, stirring constantly. Let the sauce simmer until it thickens for about 3 to 5 minutes. Once thickened, reduce the heat to low and stir in the crumbled blue cheese and grated Parmesan. Allow the cheeses to melt into the sauce, creating a smooth, creamy texture. Season with salt, black pepper, and white pepper to taste.

**Combine pasta and sauce:** Gently fold in the cooked pasta, making sure it's evenly coated with the sauce. Remove the pan from heat.

**Assemble and bake:** Preheat the oven to 375°F. Transfer the pasta and sauce mixture into a greased baking dish (or divide into smaller dishes if preferred). Top generously with shredded mozzarella. Bake for 15 to 20 minutes, or until the cheese is melted, bubbly, and lightly golden on top. Remove from the oven and enjoy.

*If you don't like blue cheese you can substitute it out for a different cheese of your choice.*

**Prep time:** 35 minutes
**Cook time:** 45 minutes

**SERVES 4**

# ORECCHIETTE WITH SAUSAGE AND BROCCOLINI

8 cloves of garlic
5 basil leaves
¼ cup olive oil
4 cups orecchiette (you can substitute penne as well)
6 broccolini, cut into 2-inch pieces (or you can leave whole)
1 tablespoon olive oil
4 Italian sausage links or 16 ounces ground Italian sausage
Pinch of red pepper flakes
3 tablespoons white wine (optional)
¾ cup chicken broth
½ cup grated Romano cheese (can substitute with Parmesan)
Salt and pepper to taste

*Broccoli can be substituted for the broccolini.*

*Orecchiette is my little brother Gabby's favorite pasta. Growing up in a restaurant family has its advantages. When Gabby was little, he asked why all his friends ate butter noodles when they could have orecchiette with creamy pesto sauce instead. Orecchiette means little ears and they are from the Adriatic side of Italy in Puglia. This dish is a perfect quick dish as it is very simple and packs lots of flavor.*

**Make garlic sauce:** In a food processor, add garlic, basil, and ¼ cup of oil; blend until the consistency of a pesto. If you don't have a blender, you can mince the garlic and basil and mix with oil in a bowl.

**Cook pasta:** Bring a large pot of water to a boil and cook orecchiette for 13 minutes or until desired texture. Make sure your water is heavily salted. Drain and rinse pasta; set aside.

**Blanch broccolini:** Bring another pot of water to a boil and blanch broccolini for about 5 minutes or until the stems are tender. Drain, rinse, and set aside.

**Make dish:** Put 1 tablespoon olive oil into pan on medium-high. If using whole Italian sausages, gently slice your Italian sausage lengthwise and take the meat out of the casing to use the ground sausage; discard casings. If you want, you can also just cut it into pieces. Sauté the sausage until browned. Add red pepper flakes and garlic sauce and sauté for about 2 minutes, taking care not to burn the garlic. Add white wine and allow to simmer for 2 minutes to cook down. Add chicken broth and brocollini; bring to a simmer.

**Finish:** Toss in the cooked pasta and cook on medium heat until it absorbs the chicken broth. Add cheese and season with salt and pepper according to your taste.

Prep time: 30 minutes
Cook time: 45 minutes

**SERVES 4**

# STEAK ALLA RUSTICA

2 tablespoons olive oil
½ yellow onion, julienned
1 green bell pepper, cut into ¼-inch x 3-inch strips
5 sundried tomatoes, cut into ¼-inch strips
10 button mushrooms, stems removed and quartered
5 cloves garlic, sliced crosswise into thin little chips
½ cup white wine
3 (1-pound, 12-ounce) cans peeled whole San Marzano tomatoes
¼ cup water
1 teaspoon dried oregano
5 basil leaves, chiffonade
1 teaspoon salt
Pinch of red pepper flakes
4 steaks of choice

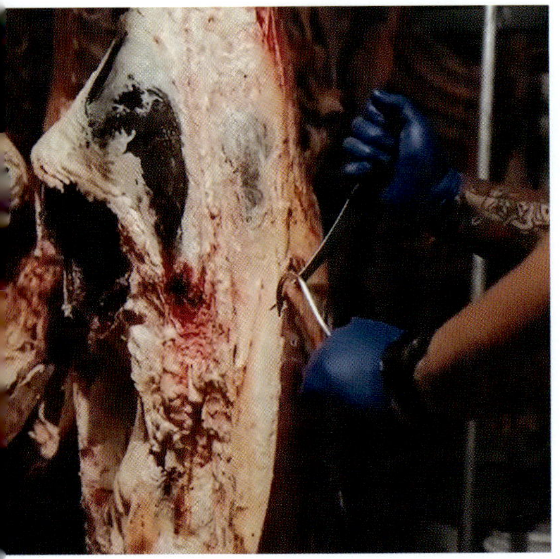

*This sauce was created by my mom as the perfect complement to the steaks at Solimene's. At the restaurant, we would sauté fresh vegetables, add a splash of wine, and then stir in our rich marinara sauce. It quickly became a favorite among our guests. While it's fantastic over steak, it also pairs wonderfully with grilled chicken or fish. For those who like a little heat, feel free to add some red pepper flakes to spice things up. This versatile sauce is perfect not only over your favorite protein, but also over pasta, making it a simple yet flavorful dish to enjoy.*

**Cook aromatics:** In a large pot, heat 2 tablespoons oil over medium-high heat. Add the chopped onion and sauté until translucent, about 4 to 5 minutes. Add the bell peppers, sundried tomatoes, and mushrooms and cook for another 2 minutes until the vegetables soften and release some of their juices.

**Infuse with garlic:** Add the sliced garlic and cook for 30 seconds to 1 minute, just until fragrant (be careful not to burn the garlic).

**Deglaze and simmer:** Pour in the white wine, stirring to deglaze the pot. Let it cook down by half, which will concentrate the flavors, about 2 to 3 minutes.

**Add tomatoes and seasoning:** Crush the canned tomatoes by hand for a rustic texture and add them to the pot along with the water, oregano, basil, salt, and red pepper flakes. Stir to combine, then lower the heat and let the sauce simmer for about 20 minutes, allowing the flavors to meld and the canned flavor of the tomatoes to cook out. Taste and adjust seasoning as needed (a pinch of sugar can help balance the acidity, if desired).

**Cook steak:** While the sauce simmers, grill or pan-fry your steak to your desired level of doneness. Rest the steak for a few minutes after cooking to retain its juices.

Spoon the savory tomato-basil sauce generously over the cooked steak and enjoy! This sauce pairs wonderfully with any cut of steak, from ribeye to flank steak.

Prep time: 15 minutes
Cook time: 2 hours

**SERVES 6**

# LAMB OSSOBUCO

6 small lamb shanks (preferably around ¾-pounds each)
Salt and pepper, for seasoning lamb
2 tablespoons olive oil
5 cloves garlic, minced
1 tablespoon chopped rosemary
Pinch of red pepper flakes
½ cup white wine
1 cup peeled canned tomatoes, hand-crushed
1½ cups beef stock
¼ cup pitted kalamata olives
1 tablespoon chopped Italian parsley

*I love lamb shank. At Solimene's, my mom always trusted me with the meats, and this dish became one of my favorites to make. The best part about it is that it holds up beautifully because of the rich fat in the shank, making it a perfect dish for the restaurant. Serving it was a breeze! The secret to a great ossobuco lies in two key steps: seasoning generously and getting a perfect sear. The meat won't brown fully in the sauce, so getting that Maillard reaction (the caramelizing of the meat) before braising is crucial to develop deep layers of flavors. This is also the perfect date night dish—if your date isn't already falling for you, they certainly will be after you serve this! It's a winner, both in flavor and presentation.*

**Season lamb:** Generously season the lamb shanks with salt and pepper on all sides.

**Brown lamb:** In a pot or Dutch oven, heat olive oil over medium-high heat. Add the lamb shanks and cook, turning occasionally, until they are browned on all sides. Once browned, pour out any excess fat from the pot.

**Sauté aromatics:** Add minced garlic, rosemary, and red pepper flakes to the pot. Cook for about 2 minutes, being careful not to burn the garlic. Pour in the wine and bring the mixture to a simmer.

**Make sauce:** Stir in the crushed tomatoes and beef stock, then reduce the heat to low. Cover the pot and let the lamb simmer, turning the shanks occasionally, for about 1.5 hours or until the lamb is fork-tender. Stir in the olives and allow them to warm through, about 5 minutes. Add parsley.

Spoon the sauce over the lamb shanks and serve with mashed potatoes or polenta for a hearty meal.

Prep time: 10 minutes
Cook time: 15 minutes

SERVES 4

# GARLIC SHRIMP AGLIO OLIO

½ box of spaghetti
Handful of garlic (around 20 cloves)
10 sweet basil leaves
Pinch of red pepper flakes
3 tablespoons olive oil
12 shrimp, peeled and deveined
Salt and pepper to taste

*This dish is simplicity at its finest. We had two cooks who started at Solimene's that have been with us forever—Chazon and Kelvin (Chazon still runs my Hawaiian BBQ restaurant). We had two types of garlic sauce that we would us. One was called "Kelvin's garlic" and was just a garlic and oil blend. The other was called "Chazon's garlic," and this is what we will be using for this dish. It is a delicious blend of garlic, herbs, and oil, and its versatility will surprise you as it can be used in sauces, for garlic bread, garlic shrimp, garlic fries, and the list goes on.*

**Cook pasta:** In a pot of heavily salted water over high heat, boil pasta to desired texture; drain and set aside.

**Make garlic sauce:** In a food processor, add garlic, basil, pepper flakes, and oil. Blend until the texture of pesto. Set aside.

**Cook shrimp:** In a pan, add oil on medium-high heat; cook shrimp until fully cooked. Remove and set aside.

**Finish sauce:** In the same pan, reduce heat to medium-low and add the garlic sauce. Cook for about 2 minutes taking care not to burn the garlic. Toss in the pasta and shrimp and season to taste.

*If you want to add a little more flavor, instead of cooking the shrimp in a pan, coat the shrimp in a little of the garlic sauce and grill them before tossing them into the pasta.*

Prep time: 25 minutes
Cook time: 20 minutes

**SERVES 4**

# LINGUINE WITH WHITE CLAM SAUCE

½ box linguine pasta
10 cloves garlic
8 basil leaves
Pinch of red pepper flakes
5 tablespoons olive oil (not extra virgin, you can also use avocado oil)
1½ cups white wine
1 cup chopped clams (3 [6-ounce] cans)
2 cups clam juice
1 teaspoon salt

3 tablespoons minced parsley
Grated Romano or Parmesan

*This was my grandpa's (who I was named after) favorite recipe. It only has a few ingredients, so making it is simple. I always found it funny that "we don't add cheese to seafood dishes" was a rule growing up. However, nothing is better than a bowl of hot linguine with clam sauce covered in grated Parmesan. Sometimes it is important to listen to traditions, but not strictly follow them, because innovation is key to moving our industry forward. This recipe is an ode to "Pops," and I know he would approve.*

**Cook pasta:** In a large pot of boiling water, season heavily with salt and boil pasta. Drain and set aside.

**Make garlic sauce:** In a food processor, add garlic, basil, red pepper flakes, and oil; blend until it is the consistency of pesto.

**Make pasta sauce:** In a pot large enough to fit all the pasta, on medium-high heat add the garlic sauce and quickly cook. DO NOT burn the garlic. Add white wine and cook for about 5 minutes until it cooks down by half. Add chopped clams, clam juice, and salt and simmer for another 5 minutes

**Finish:** Add pasta and toss in sauce, sprinkle in parsley and serve with grated Romano or Parmesan cheese.

*If you have fresh clams, feel free to throw them in. Just wash and cook separately and add them in at the end.*

# SEAFOOD FRA DIAVOLO

Prep time: 25 minutes
Cook time: 45 minutes

**SERVES 4**

Spaghetti or pasta of choice
4 cloves garlic
5 basil leaves
3 tablespoons olive oil
Pinch of salt
1 yellow onion, chopped
2 tablespoons olive oil
½ cup white wine
3 (1-pound, 12-ounce) cans San Marzano tomatoes, hand-crushed
1 tablespoon salt
1 tablespoon red pepper flakes (can use more if you want more spice)
1 teaspoon dried oregano
1 pounds cooked mussels in shells (can use raw)
1 pound cooked Manila clams (can us raw)
½ pound scallops
½ pound shrimp, peeled and deveined

*If using raw shellfish, steam or boil first until they open and are cooked before adding to the sauce.*

*Like most Italian American families, every Christmas Eve my family does the Feast of Seven Fishes. Before I was born, my mom has been making this fiery New York-style sauce to cook a majority of our seafood in one dish. It has become such a tradition that my little brother refuses to do anything else for Christmas Eve! Translated to "brother devil," obviously this dish has a spicy kick to it, so be careful and adjust accordingly. You don't have to be handcuffed to these seafood either. Feel free to add lobster, calamari, fish, or whatever you like. From my Italian family to yours, I hope you enjoy our traditional holiday meal.*

**Cook pasta:** In a pot, add water heavily seasoned with salt, bring to a boil and cook pasta to desired texture. Set aside.

**Blend aromatics:** In a food processor, add garlic, basil, and 3 tablespoons of olive oil with a pinch of salt and blend until the consistency of pesto. Set aside. In a food processor, add chunks of onion and blend until smooth.

**Cook sauce:** In a pot over medium-high heat, add 2 tablespoons of olive oil and add onions. Cook until liquid evaporates. Add garlic sauce and cook another 3 minutes. Add white wine and bring to a simmer. Add San Marzano tomatoes (hand-crush them as you add), salt, red pepper flakes, and oregano and allow to slowly cook for about 20 minutes until the flavor of the can has cooked out.

**Cook seafood:** Add mussels and clams and cook for about 5 minutes. Next add shrimp and cook for an additional 5 minutes. And finally, add scallops, cooking for 5 more minutes or until all seafood is fully cooked.

Serve over pasta with grated Parmesan.

Prep time: 20 minutes
Cook time: 35 minutes

**SERVES 4**

# SEARED SCALLOPS AND SUNDRIED TOMATO CREAM SAUCE

3 cloves garlic
8 sundried tomatoes
10 basil leaves
¾ cup grated Romano cheese (can use Parmesan), divided use
½ cup olive oil (if you can use the oil from the sundried tomato, use that)
Pinch of salt
2 cups of penne pasta
1¼ cups cream
1 tablespoon avocado oil or neutral oil
12 scallops

*I can still picture those nights when I was just out of culinary school and back home with my girlfriend (who would eventually become my wife). After long shifts at Solimene's, we'd unwind with a comforting bowl of pasta—pesto cream sauce paired with either scallops or shrimp. We'd park in my parents' empty lot, watch* **The Sopranos** *on my laptop, and savor one of my favorite dishes. There's something about the way this meal comes together: the creamy richness, the tangy depth of sundried tomatoes, and the fresh brightness of basil. It's a dish that never fails to deliver a sense of comfort, warmth, and nostalgia—a true winner every time.*

**Make pesto:** In a food processor, combine the garlic, sundried tomatoes, basil, ¼ cup Romano cheese, olive oil, and a pinch of salt. Blend until the mixture reaches a pesto-like consistency. Set aside.

**Cook pasta:** Bring a large pot of salted water to a boil. Cook the pasta until it reaches your desired level of doneness. Drain and set aside.

**Make sauce:** In a large pot, heat the pesto mixture over medium heat for about 3 minutes. Add the cream and the remaining ½ cup of Romano cheese. Reduce the heat to medium. Once it comes to a simmer, mix it well and turn heat off. Make sure not to cook too long or your sauce might separate Season with freshly ground black pepper to taste.

**Combine pasta and sauce:** Toss the cooked pasta into the sauce and mix until well-coated. Turn off the heat.

**Sear scallops:** In a nonstick pan, heat 1 tablespoon of olive oil over medium-high heat. Pat the scallops dry with a paper towel and season them with salt and pepper. Sear the scallops for about 3 minutes on each side, or until golden brown and caramelized.

Plate the pasta and top with the seared scallops. Drizzle with the sundried tomato cream sauce and serve immediately.

# THE THREE FAT PIGS

## *Perfect Imperfections*

We all know the saying "when it rains it pours," and this was never more accurate as it was on the opening day of The Three Fat Pigs. Our goals and dreams always seem nice and tidy floating around in our subconscious minds, but sometimes those dreams can turn into nightmares. That is what it felt like to me on opening night as the Waikoloa moon shone bright through the dining room windows. This story starts off like every other, with our main character walking blindly into issue after issue until everything is resolved and the arc turns back down to the happily ever after.

This was the Big island's first ever gastropub, and I was young and ambitious, so my menu had a mix of classic dishes with modern molecular gastronomy techniques.

The night started off as most of my opening nights. I was expecting a few issues, but the excitement and anticipation of success suppressed my nerves. This was the Big island's first ever gastropub, and I was young and ambitious, so my menu had a mix of classic dishes with modern molecular gastronomy techniques—foams, spherification, emulsions, etc. I would say I was excited, but that would be the wrong word. Nauseous would be more accurate. I was prepared though, this being the second restaurant I opened and the fourth that my family had opened. I was expecting the bumps.

Everything started off great. I had an experienced sous chef, an eager kitchen crew, and a fantastic front crew albeit green. We already made it through the soft opening so the major kinks were worked out. But on opening night, you should always expect the unexpected.

We were fully booked and our reservations were at capacity. I created the menu to have quicker pickup times as there were close to 100 seats in the restaurant. It was two stories, with a large mural over the open kitchen of three pigs in the art style of Beatrice Potter (Peter Rabbit) that I had contracted to fit the whimsical theme of the restaurant. The upstairs bar and lounge were named The Thirsty Wolf lounge and offered a bar snack menu and intricate, yet borderline pretentious, drink menu. The space was beautiful, open, and modern.

The first few orders went out status quo. The wheels seemed to be turning and the machine that is a restaurant was rolling along as planned. About halfway through the dinner service, my sous chef approached me and told me that he was going to head home. I told him that it was only 8 p.m. and he said that he was too old to stay late at night. I knew I would have to let him go. With no sous chef and myself expediting, we were still on the right path, but the path had gotten a bit bumpy. While I was calling out orders and directing my food runner to tables with trays full of food,

**At only twenty-three years old, I learned that if you don't go with the flow, you will drown. Like all the restaurants we opened, I laced up my steel-toed nonslip shoes the next day and went in ready to fix the problems and face the new ones.**

my bartender approached me. He said that the floor drain behind the bar was starting to back up and water, mixed with dirt and grease, was coming back up. We stuffed a few towels into the floor drain hoping this quick fix was going to hold until the plumber could come in the next day, a bad decision in the long run, but hindsight is 20/20. The shopping center we were in was old, and it is fair to say that the plumbing needed some work. The problem had a band aid on it when what it really needed was stitches. I started to panic a bit as I knew the smell would soon follow this greasy water, and we still had a couple hours of service to get through. As we cooked our way through the next few orders, the floor drain in the back of the kitchen started to overflow as well. It was at this point I knew we had to cut off walk-ins and just finish the last of our customers with reservations. That is when one of my green servers walked up to me on the line and said, "Chef, the food critic for *Honolulu Magazine* is here and wants to know what you recommend for dessert."

My eyes got wide and I bit my bottom lip, trying to keep myself from screaming. I asked the server why they didn't inform me when the critic first came in, and they said they just got "too busy." This is when it all hit me like a freight train. I dropped to a squat so that the customers couldn't see me and started to feel the pressure building up. I am a lifer, someone who has been in the restaurant industry their whole lives, so I am used to solving problems un-

der pressure. But these problems were out of my control. I walked outside and my wife saw me from her post at the hostess stand and helped to calm me down. This is the part of the dream when you are falling and either wake up before you hit the ground or fly. I chose fly. I went back in and picked out our best dessert, took it to the food critic, and with the best charm I could muster, explained to her my concept and inspiration for the restaurant. She must have been understanding because I didn't get any questions about the smell that was only now wafting into the dining room. She thanked me and left, and we proceeded to close out the rest of the customers and clear the dining room.

Lessons in life are only learned through failure. If you don't experience problems, you will never know how to solve them. The review came out and it was not at all what I expected. The food critic praised the creativity of the concept. It also helped me grow as a chef. At only twenty-three years old, I learned that if you don't go with the flow, you will drown. Like all the restaurants we opened, I laced up my steel-toed nonslip shoes the next day and went in ready to fix the problems and face the new ones.

I am forever grateful to The Three Fat Pigs as it truly helped me grow as a chef and restaurateur. I learned there that you are not cooking for yourself but for your target demographic, and if you allow your ego to get in the way, you will ultimately fail. It has been thirteen years since that opening night, and the vivid lessons have stuck with me till this day. I loved that restaurant and the food we put out. Although I had some ups and downs, I wouldn't trade it for anything. I am also grateful for my family. Without them, I would never have made it as far as I have. The Three Fat Pigs might not be here today, but everything that transpired has turned me into the chef I am and for that I am grateful.

Prep time: 20 minutes
Cook time: 30 minutes

SERVES 4

# SMOKED GOUDA CHEESE SAUCE WITH HOMEMADE CHIPS

2 tablespoons unsalted butter
2 tablespoons all-purpose flour
1 cup milk
1⅓ cups grated smoked Gouda
1 teaspoon Tabasco
1 teaspoon Worcestershire sauce
5 Yukon Gold potatoes
Pinch of salt
2 teaspoons white vinegar

*Nothing is better than a homemade potato chip, unless that homemade potato chip is served with a smoked cheese sauce! This was one of my bar menu items at The Three Fat Pigs, because not only does it satisfy, it keeps people drinking more. Homemade potato chips take a few more steps than just slicing and frying. You could do that, but there is too much sugar and they will get dark and a bit bitter. Follow these steps and you will never go back to store bought potato chips again. Controlling the starch content is key, and that is why we rinse, boil, and dry. Enjoy this appetizer with a nice cold beer or glass of wine.*

*You can use a different cheese instead of smoked Gouda. Mozzarella or blue cheese also work well.*

**Make sauce:** In a sauce pot over medium heat, melt butter and mix in flour. Cook for about 5 minutes. Pour in milk and whisk well. While continuing to whisk, bring it to a simmer, allowing it to thicken. Slowly add cheese while mixing to melt and incorporate all the cheese. Once smooth and well-mixed, stir in Tabasco and Worcestershire.

**Make chips:** Rinse off Yukon Gold potatoes, slice them thin (you can go as thin as 1/16 to ⅛-inch thick) on a mandolin into a bowl of water. Once they are all sliced, pour out water and keep rinsing until the water runs clear.

In a sauce pot, add sliced potatoes and cover with water. Add a pinch of salt and white vinegar. Bring to a boil. As soon as it starts boiling, set timer for 5 minutes. Once boiled, pour sliced potatoes into a colander and rinse with water until they are cooled.

Line a sheet pan or a plate with paper towels, place each potato chip down onto the paper towels without overlapping them. Place another paper towel on top and repeat the process until finished. This step is important as you must get most of the water out.

Preheat oil to 325°F. In batches, cook the potato chips until they are golden and crispy. Salt them immediately so the salt sticks to them and pour them into a paper towel lined bowl and allow to cool.

Serve with the cheese sauce.

Prep time: 10 minutes
Cook time: 10 minutes

**SERVES 4**

# SPRING SALAD WITH CHAMPAGNE VINAIGRETTE

½ cup mayonnaise
1 tablespoon Dijon mustard
1 tablespoon honey
2½ tablespoons champagne vinegar (can use white vinegar)
1½ teaspoons fresh black pepper, cracked
Salt to taste
8 pieces of asparagus
3 heads butter lettuce
3 tablespoons goat cheese
¼ cup of peas
¼ red onion, julienned
3 tablespoons sunflower seeds

*This salad might seem fancy, but it is very easy and tasty. We would serve this salad on our spring menu at The Three Fat Pigs. The creamy tanginess of the dressing paired with the fresh crunch of asparagus and peas are a perfect balance. Serve this salad with a grilled piece of fish, chicken breast, or on its own.*

---

**Make dressing:** In a mixing bowl, add mayonnaise, Dijon, honey, champagne vinegar, pepper, and whisk together. Season with salt to taste.

**Blanch asparagus:** In a saucepan, bring water to a boil and drop in asparagus for between 3 to 5 minutes until asparagus is tender but still has some bite. Drain and run under water until cool. Slice the asparagus into 1-inch pieces.

**Assemble:** Chop lettuce and top with goat cheese, peas, asparagus, onion, sunflower seeds and dressing.

Prep time: 15 minutes
Cook time: 1½ hours (including pickling)

SERVES 4

# BLTA (BACON, LETTUCE, PICKLED TOMATO, AND AVOCADO) SANDWICH

½ cup red wine vinegar
¼ cup water
1 teaspoon pickling spice
¼ cup white sugar
1 clam shell of cherry tomatoes, cut in half (about 1 cup)
2 tablespoons unsalted butter
8 slices sourdough (or any sliced bread you prefer)
16 slices bacon
3 tablespoons mayonnaise
2 teaspoons Dijon mustard
8 green leaf lettuce
¼ red onion, thinly sliced
1 avocado, sliced

*You can store your tomatoes in an airtightcontainer for up to a week in the refrigerator.*

*I'm a self-proclaimed pickle fanatic—making them is one of my absolute favorite things to do in the kitchen. So, when I was putting together my lunch menu, I knew I wanted to reinvent the classic BLT. I wanted to give it a unique twist, and pickling the cherry tomatoes became the perfect solution. The subtle acidity from the pickled tomatoes cuts through the richness of the crispy bacon, creating a beautiful balance of flavors. This small tweak adds a delightful pop of brightness to every bite, and I guarantee it will quickly become your new favorite way to enjoy a BLT. It's the perfect combination of familiar comfort and a fresh, tangy twist that's sure to elevate your lunchtime experience.*

**Pickle tomato:** In a small saucepan, add red wine vinegar, water, pickling spice, and sugar and bring to a boil. Once boiling, turn off heat and add cherry tomatoes. Allow to cool and refrigerate for at least an hour or overnight.

**Prepare sandwich:** Preheat pan to medium, butter each side of bread, and toast in the pan until golden on each side; set aside.

**Cook bacon:** In a nonstick pan over medium heat, add bacon slices and cook on each side until desired doneness. Some like extra crispy bacon, some like it a little less crispy.

Alternatively, set your oven to 400°F and place your bacon on a sheet pan lined with parchment paper (you can use tinfoil instead if you don't have parchment). Bake in the oven for about 20 to 30 minutes, checking often after 15 minutes, because not all bacon is cut the same. Once crispy, remove from pan and place on a paper towel-lined plate.

**Assemble sandwich:** In a small bowl, mix the mayonnaise and Dijon mustard together and smear on one side of each toasted bread. Place down 2 lettuce leaves, a spoonful of your pickled cherry tomatoes, sliced red onion, avocado, and bacon.

# MISO RISOTTO

Prep time: 15 minutes
Cook time: 45 minutes

SERVES 4

- 9 cups water
- 1 tablespoon Hon Dashi granules
- 6 ounces white miso paste
- ½ yellow onion, minced
- 1 tablespoon minced ginger
- 3 cloves garlic, minced
- 2 cups Arborio rice
- ¼ cup sake
- ¼ cup grated Romano cheese (optional)
- 1 tablespoon minced parsley

*Another great dish you can create with the miso risotto is arancini. Let the risotto sit in the refrigerator overnight. Scoop small amounts and roll them into balls. Roll the balls in beaten egg, then panko, and deep fry them to create a miso arancini ball like no other.*

*I learned how to make risotto while on a boat in Italy by a large Italian chef whose name escapes me. His advice was to always use a wine (sake in this recipe) and make sure that the broth you are using is very hot to release the starch. I enjoy using miso because not only does it add to the creaminess, but the subtle fermented flavor creates the same flavor profile as cheese without using any dairy. This dish is like eating a bowl of miso soup and is a combination of cuisines I grew up with—Japanese food and Italian. I call it Euro-Pacific cuisine.*

**Make broth:** In a pot over high heat, bring water to a boil. Add Hon Dashi and miso and whisk well. Turn down to low heat.

**Cook aromatics:** In a separate pan, sauté onions until translucent. Add ginger and garlic and cook another 2 minutes.

**Start risotto:** Add Arborio rice and cook another 3 minutes allowing rice to toast. Pour sake over rice and allow it to cook down (about 5 minutes). Once sake is cooked down by half, start ladling in miso soup 6 ounces at a time. Keep stirring. This part is important because the creaminess comes from the breaking up of the starch, so don't stop stirring. As liquid evaporates, add more and continue this process until the rice is tender (about 35 minutes, but taste for texture). Once rice is cooked add cheese and parsley; stir. You might not use all the broth, so keep tasting to check the texture of the rice, making sure it is cooked through.

If you want it to be vegan, you can omit the cheese.

Prep time: 30 minutes
Cook time: 45 minutes

**SERVES 4**

# COCONUT CURRY CHICKEN POT PIE

1 tablespoon neutral oil
3 chicken thighs, skinless and boneless, cut into bite-size pieces
½ onion, chopped
1 carrot, diced small
3 stalks celery, diced small
2 tablespoons green curry paste
1 (14-ounce) can coconut milk
1 cup vegetable broth
2 makrut lime leaf (optional)
3 teaspoons white sugar
1 russet potato, diced
Squeeze fresh lime juice
5 Thai basil leaves, chopped
2 Japanese eggplants, diced
Salt to taste
4 puff pastry dough sheets
1 egg

*Who doesn't love a good chicken pot pie and a good curry? Why not put them together? That is what we did at The Three Fat Pigs, and the result was a popular mainstay on the menu. The best part about this dish, like a majority of my recipes, is the versatility. You can substitute the chicken for shrimp or an assortment of your favorite vegetables. Sometimes, I even add pineapple chunks to create bites of tangy sweetness. The possibilities are endless. Obviously, you don't have to make it into a pot pie. Just omit the puff pastry for a delicious coconut curry that can be served over a bowl of rice or tossed with noodles. A family favorite in my house.*

**Brown chicken:** In a large pot, heat oil over medium-high heat and brown chicken.

**Cook aromatics:** Add onion, carrots, and celery and sauté for 3 minutes or until onions are translucent. Add the green curry and cook another 3 minutes to allow curry paste to caramelize.

**Start curry:** Add coconut milk and simmer for 5 minutes. Add vegetable broth, lime leaf, and sugar and bring back to a simmer. Cook until carrots start to get soft.

Turn to a low simmer and add potatoes, lime juice, and Thai basil. Cook for another 15 minutes or until potatoes are soft. Add eggplant and cook for another 10 minutes until tender. Season with salt to taste.

**Prepare puff pastry:** Preheat oven to 400°F. Take out 4 round baking ramekins and turn them upside down onto the puff pastry sheet. Using the ramekins as a guide, cut a circle in the puff pastry about a ½-inch larger than the circumference of the ramekin. This extra ½-inch is important because the pastry will shrink in size.

Portion the curry into the four ramekins and place puff pastry over the top, tucking the edges into the ramekin. Gently score the top (don't cut all the way through).

Whip the egg to create an egg wash and gently brush the tops of each pastry to help the pastry brown.

**Bake:** Place ramekins on a cooking sheet, place in oven and bake for about 20 minutes or until the pastry is puffed up and golden. Serve immediately.

Prep time: 25 minutes
Cook time: 35 minutes

SERVES 4

# STEAK SALAD WITH CURRY PEANUT VINAIGRETTE

1 tablespoon red curry paste
¾ cup smooth peanut butter
¼ cup white sugar
2 teaspoons Aloha Shoyu
1 teaspoon salt
2 tablespoons apple cider vinegar
¾ cup water
1 lime, juiced
¼ cup coconut milk
¼ cup sweet chili sauce
2 cloves garlic
1 tablespoon minced ginger
3 New York steaks
2 heads green leaf lettuce
1 avocado, cubed
Small handful of cherry tomatoes
Small handful of cilantro, torn
¼ red onion, julienned

*This versatile salad dressing works perfectly as both a dressing and a dipping sauce. I created this recipe alongside my sous chef, Simon, envisioning a steak salad featuring a flavorful curry vinaigrette—and this is the delicious result. The addition of peanut butter gives the dressing a creamy, well-balanced texture that complements the richness of the steak beautifully. As always, feel free to get creative! Switch up the toppings, or swap the steak for chicken or fish—make it your own. The best part? The tasty rewards that come with it. Enjoy!*

**Make dressing:** Put curry, peanut butter, sugar, Aloha Shoyu, salt, apple vinegar, water, lime, coconut milk, sweet chili sauce, garlic, and ginger into a blender or food processor and blend until smooth.

**Cook steak:** Season steaks with salt and pepper. Preheat grill and cook on each side for about 8 minutes or until it is cooked to your liking. You can also cook in a hot pan. Just heat pan to medium-high, sear on each side, and put in oven on 400°F until fully cooked. Let steak rest.

**Assemble salad:** To assemble salad, chop green leaf lettuce and place on plate. Top with Curry Peanut Vinaigrette, avocado, cherry tomatoes, cilantro, and red onions. Cut steak against the grain and fan out over salad.

Prep time: 3 hours (including marinating)
Cook time: 4 hours

SERVES 4

# KOREAN BRAISED SHORT RIBS

2 cups water
1½ cups sugar
2 cups Aloha Shoyu
1 tablespoon toasted sesame oil
1 teaspoon sambal oelek
3 cloves garlic, minced
1 tablespoon minced ginger
¼ cup chopped green onion
¼ cup toasted sesame seeds
1 tablespoon neutral oil
4 pounds beef short ribs

*Who doesn't love a good short rib? Braised short ribs are a restaurant's favorite for good reason—they hold up beautifully in the sauce and can be plated in no time. Short ribs are full of fat and connective tissue. This can be used to your advantage if cooked long enough, because it adds so much more flavor when it breaks down and melts. These Korean short ribs are bursting with umami and rich flavor. With their melt-in-your-mouth tenderness, they make the perfect dish for a date night or family dinner, sure to impress everyone at the table.*

**Make sauce:** In a pot over high heat, bring the water to a boil and turn off. Whisk in the sugar until melted. Add Aloha Shoyu, sesame oil, sambal oelek, garlic, ginger, green onion, and sesame seeds and mix well.

Preheat oven to 350°F.

**Sear meat:** Heat a sauté pan over medium-high heat and add oil. Season the short ribs with salt and pepper and sear on all sides until nice and browned.

**Braise meat:** In a large baking dish, add short ribs and sauce. Make sure sauce is at least halfway up the short ribs. If it is not, add a little more water. Cover with tinfoil and place in preheated oven for about 3½ hours until the short ribs are soft enough to eat with only a fork.

Pull ribs right out of the braising liquid and serve over mashed potatoes, rice, or polenta.

*You can eat short ribs right away, or you can add the sauce to a pot and use a cornstarch slurry (1 tablespoon cornstarch + 3 tablespoons water) to thicken it.*

Prep time: 15 minutes
Cook time: 2 hours

SERVES 4

# BAVETTE WITH TOMATO FIVE SPICE JAM

- 4 large beefsteak tomatoes
- 4 cups water plus 1 cup
- 4 tablespoons white sugar
- 2 teaspoons Chinese five-spice powder
- 3 pounds bavette, or skirt steak or flank steak
- Salt and pepper

*The number of times that I have been asked for my Tomato Five Spice Jam recipe seems to be infinite. So, it is only right for me to put it in this cookbook. To say this sauce can be used on everything is an understatement. I have used this jam over seafood, steaks, pork, and even on a bagel with cream cheese! I created this dish at The Three Fat Pigs to give steak that deep flavor like a braised short rib. Feel free to use any cut of meat you like. The bavette is a cut from the bottom of the sirloin near the flank steak and is prized for its rich deep flavor and tender texture. Unless you are going to a butcher, it is not something you'll find in most grocery stores, so the closest cut would be skirt steak.*

*This jam can be made ahead of time and stored for up to two weeks in the refrigerator; serve at room temperature.*

**Make tomato jam:** In a large pot, bring water to a boil. Cut an X on the bottom of each tomato and drop them into the boiling water for a few minutes until the skin starts to peel. Pull tomatoes out and drop into cold water to stop the cooking. Peel each tomato and cut into quarters. Cut out the seeds and center of tomato.

In a sauce pan over medium-high heat, add 2 cups of water and bring to a boil. Add tomatoes, sugar, and Chinese five-spice powder; bring to a simmer. Allow the jam to simmer until liquid is half way reduced, then add another 2 cups of water. Repeat this process until liquid is reduced again. Finally, add the last cup of water and reduce while breaking up the tomato with a wooden spoon. You should have a nice chutney consistency, if not add a little more water and simmer until liquid is reduced. If you want a smoother jam, blend in a food processor. Because the seeds are removed,

you won't get that bitter flavor that comes with breaking the tomato seed.

**Cook meat:** Preheat your grill till hot (at least 400°F). Bring steak to room temperature and season with salt and pepper. Cook bavette over hot grill for about 5 minutes on each side until it is done the way you like it (bavette and skirt steak are the most tender at medium-rare).

To serve, slice meat against the grain and top with Tomato Five Spice Jam.

Prep time: 30 minutes (plus 3 hours to marinate)
Cook time: 30 minutes

SERVES 4

# POMEGRANATE AND CORIANDER GLAZED RACK OF LAMB

2 tablespoons coriander seeds
2 teaspoons cumin seeds
Pinch of salt
3 cloves garlic
1 tablespoon olive oil
6 tablespoons pomegranate molasses reduction
1 tablespoon balsamic reduction
4 racks of lamb, cleaned and Frenched

*To make balsamic reduction, add 1 cup balsamic to a small saucepan and slowly simmer until the vinegar lightly sticks to the back of a spoon. Do not overcook as this can burn. You can do the same thing for pomegranate molasses; just use pomegranate juice instead of balsamic vinegar.*

*Lamb can be a polarizing dish—people either love it or dislike it. Those who aren't fans often mention the strong gamey flavor, but this recipe helps to balance that with a tangy pomegranate and balsamic reduction. The acidity from the reduction works wonders in cutting through the gamey taste, creating the perfect flavor combination. I've used this technique with other game meats as well, and it's always a hit. However, lamb remains my favorite way to enjoy this recipe.*

**Make marinade:** Toast the coriander and cumin in a pan until fragrant. Using a mortar and pestle grind, the coriander and cumin with a pinch of salt. Add garlic and smash into a paste. Add olive oil, pomegranate, and balsamic reduction and mix together. Marinate the lamb for at least 3 hours (preferably overnight).

**Cook lamb:** Get a grill hot and cook each side of the lamb until nice a caramelized. Internal temperature should reach 145°F.

Serve with your favorite vegetable. If you have any extra reduction or molasses, drizzle a little over the meat.

Prep time: 30 minutes
Cook time: 3 hours

**SERVES 4**

# BRAISED LAMB LEG IN TOMATO RAGU

- 2 tablespoons neutral oil
- 1 teaspoon cumin seeds
- 1 yellow onion, minced
- 2 large dried whole chilies (can substitute for 2 teaspoons red pepper flakes)
- 4 cloves garlic, minced
- 2 tablespoons minced ginger
- 2 cardamom pods
- 4 cloves
- 4 pound boneless lamb leg (can use a 5 pound bone-in leg)
- 2 pounds tomatoes, quartered
- 1½ teaspoons garam masala
- Pinch of salt
- 2 teaspoons white sugar
- Boiling water

*This dish has a similar vibe to my oxtail stew, fragrant and warming. I love lamb, but the gamey flavor can turn off many people. This is my remedy to that. Packed with so much flavor, the umami and acid from the tomatoes and the warmth of the spices helps to cut through that game flavor and create a beautiful dish that not just fills the belly but warms the soul.*

**Sear aromatics:** Heat oil in a large pot over medium-high heat. Add cumin seeds and cook for 2 minutes. Add onions, chilies, garlic, and ginger and sauté for 5 minutes.

**Brown meat:** Add cardamom and cloves. Add lamb chunks and cook for another 5 minutes, searing all sides. Add tomatoes and garam masala. Once the tomatoes get soft and their skin starts to loosen, turn heat down and add enough boiling water to cover everything. Bring to a simmer and add a pinch of salt; reduce heat to low.

**Braise meat:** Cover and simmer for 2 hours, stirring often to make sure it doesn't stick to the bottom of the pot (add additional water if needed). Once finished, add sugar. It should be the consistency of a thick stew.

Serve over pasta, rice, or with some toasted bread.

**Prep time:** 15 minutes
**Cook time:** 3 hours

**SERVES 4**

# OXTAIL STEW

- 2 tablespoons neutral oil, divided use
- 4 pounds oxtail
- 1 gallon water
- 2 cinnamon sticks
- 4 star anise
- 2 tablespoons salt
- 1 onion, quartered
- 2 carrots, cut into 2-inch chunks
- 3 stalks celery, cut into 1-inch pieces
- 3 cloves garlic, smashed
- 3 pounds peeled canned tomatoes, hand-crushed
- 1 teaspoon black pepper
- 5 basil leaves, minced
- 3 cups oxtail broth
- 5 Yukon Gold potatoes, quartered

*In the restaurant, I would serve this stew with a dollop of sour cream on top and a side of cornbread.*

*I created this dish as a fusion of two of my favorite flavors—oxtail soup and tripe stew. The addition of cinnamon and star anise imparts a unique and delightful warmth and depth of flavor. Oxtail has always been one of my favorite cuts of meat, versatile enough to be used in countless dishes. When cooked properly, the flavor and texture of oxtail are simply unmatched. This hybrid recipe is the ultimate oxtail dish—one you'll never need another for.*

---

**Make broth:** In a large pot over medium-high heat, add 1 tablespoon oil and sear each oxtail until golden brown. Add water, cinnamon sticks, anise, and salt. Simmer partially covered for at least 2 hours, until the oxtail is fork tender. Drain, but reserve 3 cups of the liquid (oxtail broth). Remove oxtails from pot and set them aside.

**Cook aromatics:** In the same large pot, add 1 tablespoon oil over medium-high heat and sauté the onions, carrots, and celery until fragrant for about 5 minutes. Add garlic cloves and cook an additional 2 minutes.

**Make stew:** Add the crushed tomatoes, pepper, and basil and slowly simmer for 30 minutes. Add 3 cups of oxtail broth and oxtails and simmer for additional 20 minutes. Add potatoes last and cook until potatoes are fork tender. If your stew is too thick, you can add a little more oxtail broth. Season to taste.

Prep time: 15 minutes
Cook time: 45 minutes

**SERVES 4**

# KANPACHI EN PAPILLOTE

- 4 skinless kanpachi fillets, cut to 6-ounce portions
- 1 large piece of ginger, peeled and sliced into thin matchsticks (julienne slice)
- 2 cups whole cilantro leaves
- 8 teaspoons sake
- 8 teaspoons Aloha Shoyu
- 12 tablespoons sesame oil
- Parchment Paper

*You can substitute the kanpachi for any white fish that you prefer. Make sure to remove the skin as this technique will tend to make it soggy.*

*En papillote translates to "in paper" in French. I love using this cooking technique, because it gently steams the fish, locking in all the flavors and leaving the fish moist and incredibly flavorful. This dish combines two different techniques: the French papillote method and a quick flash-fry using hot sesame oil—a technique commonly used in Chinese cooking. I enjoy blending these cultures. Having grown up in Hawai'i, I'm surrounded by Chinese influences, yet my background in a French culinary school has instilled in me a deep appreciation for the precision and technique of French cooking. This dish is designed to be both simple and elegant—perfect for impressing someone on a date night.*

Preheat oven to 400°F.

**Assemble packets:** Cut off 4 squares of parchment that are at least 12 inches on each side. Lay the sheet flat on a work surface. Place one fish fillet on a sheet and place ¼ of the ginger and ¼ cup of cilantro leaves on top of the fish. Then pour 2 teaspoons sake and 2 teaspoons Aloha Shoyu over everything.

Lift the right and left sides of the paper up and towards the center, directly above the fish. Touch the two sides together and tightly roll them, folding as you go, until you reach the fish. Now, roll and crimp the top and bottom ends, rolling them towards the counter, away from the center of the fish. When you reach the ends of the fish, tuck the ends underneath the fish. Place the packet on a rimmed baking sheet, using the weight of the fish to hold the ends in place. You don't want the packet to come unsealed as it bakes. Repeat with remaining three packets.

**Cook fish:** Bake for about 12 minutes until cooked through. Once fish is cooked, leave on sheet pan and rip the packet open.

In a sauce pan, heat sesame oil until smoking. Take 3 tablespoons of hot sesame oil and pour over the cilantro, ginger, and fish to "flash-fry" the fish. Repeat until all the fish is done.

Remove everything from the parchment paper packets. You can discard the ginger and cilantro or leave it on.

Serve over hot rice or a salad.

Prep time: 20 minutes
Cook time: 30 minutes (plus 3 hours for pickles)

**SERVES 4**

# SHICHIMI BLACKENED SALMON WITH VIETNAMESE-STYLE PICKLES

*I have done many cooking competitions and created a few recipes that would make it to my restaurant's menu. This is one of those recipes. Shichimi translates to "seven-flavor chili pepper" and can be traced to the Edo period in Japan. You can find this little jar in most ramen restaurants, and it packs some serious flavor. This rub can be a bit spicy, so if you aren't as into spice, feel free to add more brown sugar to your rub. As much as you will enjoy the salmon, I personally believe that the pickles will steal the show in this dish.*

- ¼ cup Aloha Shoyu
- ¼ cup fish sauce (patis)
- ¼ cup rice vinegar
- ¼ cup water
- ½ tablespoon white sugar
- 1 lime, juiced and zest
- 2 tablespoons chopped cilantro
- 1 teaspoon sambal oelek
- 1 Japanese cucumber, sliced in thin rounds
- 4 tablespoons Japanese shichimi
- 2 tablespoons brown sugar
- Pinch of salt
- 4 salmon fillets, skinless
- 1 tablespoon neutral oil

**Make pickles:** In a bowl, mix Aloha Shoyu, fish sauce, vinegar, water, white sugar, lime, cilantro, and sambal and mix until sugar dissolves. Toss in cucumbers and refrigerate for at least 3 hours.

**Cook salmon:** Mix shichimi, brown sugar, and pinch of salt in a bowl. Generously season each salmon. Preheat oven to 400°F. Heat an ovenproof pan to medium-high and add oil. Once oil is hot, sear salmon on all sides and place in oven for about 10 minutes or until salmon reaches 145°F.

Take a few pickled cucumber out of the brine and place on salmon. Serve over hot jasmine rice.

*Pickles will last up to one week in the refrigerator.*

Prep time: 30 minutes
Cook time: 1 hour

**SERVES 4**

# BLACKENED 'AHI WITH PICKLED FENNEL AND HERBED YOGURT

1 fennel bulb, sliced thin
½ cup water
½ cup white sugar
1½ cups white wine vinegar
¼ cup brown sugar
¼ cup paprika
1 tablespoon ground black pepper
1 tablespoon salt
1 tablespoon chili powder
1 tablespoon garlic powder
1 tablespoon onion powder
1 tablespoon neutral oil
2 pounds 'ahi, cut into 2 blocks
½ cup Greek yogurt
1 tablespoon minced parsley
1 tablespoon minced cilantro
2 teaspoons minced dill
5 mint leaves, minced
Pinch of salt

*While this recipe is a bit more "elevated" compared to the others in this book, it's one I created to showcase our fresh 'ahi in a new and exciting way. The combination of yogurt, blackened 'ahi, and pickled fennel brings together layers of flavor that are truly unique. Traditionally, 'ahi is served with ponzu or shoyu and wasabi, but this dish offers a distinct twist. I often use it as my go-to appetizer for larger events, as everything can be prepared ahead of time and stored in the refrigerator until ready to serve. I hope this creative take on seared 'ahi offers something fresh and memorable to your table*

**Pickle fennel:** Slice fennel into thin strips. In a sauce pot over medium-high heat, add water, white sugar, and vinegar and bring to a boil. As soon as it boils, add the fennel and turn off heat. Set aside until it reaches room temperature.

**Make seasoning:** In a bowl, mix brown sugar, paprika, black pepper, salt, chili powder, garlic powder, and onion powder. Set aside.

**Blacken 'ahi:** Preheat a sauté pan over medium-high heat and add 1 tablespoon oil. Roll 'ahi in blackening seasoning to coat well and sear quickly on each side (about 2 minutes on each side). Set in refrigerator until cool.

**Make yogurt:** In a bowl, mix Greek yogurt, parsley, cilantro, dill, mint leaves, and salt; mix well.

**Assemble:** Spread yogurt sauce on a platter. Slice the ʻahi, and place on top of the yogurt sauce. Top with pickled fennel and serve.

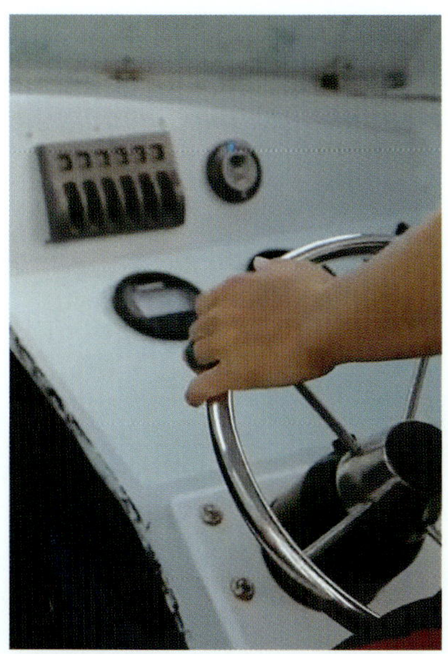

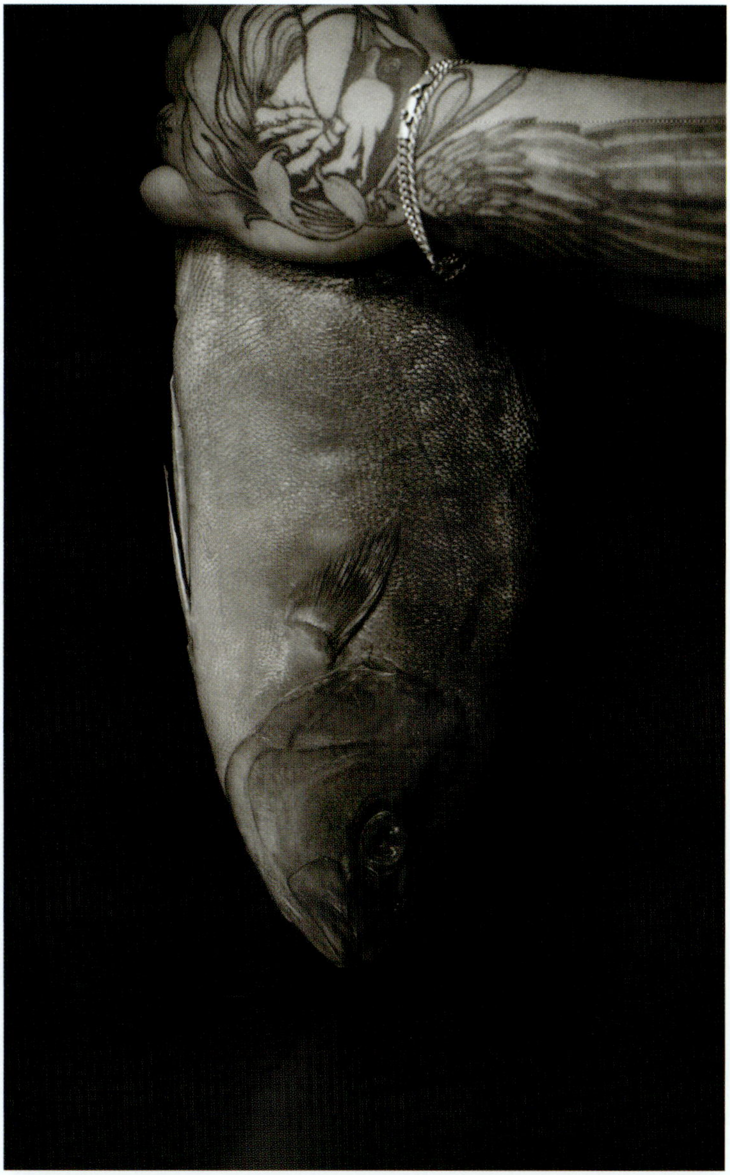

Prep time: 10 minutes
Cook time: 15 minutes

SERVES 4

# CRAB CAKES WITH WASABI AIOLI

1¼ cups mayonnaise, divided use
1 tablespoon Dijon mustard
1 tablespoon Worcestershire sauce
1 large egg, beaten
1 teaspoon Old Bay Seasoning
1 pound lump crabmeat
1 cup panko breadcrumbs
1½ tablespoons chopped parsley
1 teaspoon lemon zest
½ teaspoon salt
½ teaspoon black pepper
¼ cup canola oil
2 tablespoons wasabi paste

*Crab cakes are a beloved dish enjoyed worldwide, but what truly makes a great crab cake is the crab itself. It may sound simple, but far too often, crab cakes are filled with too much "filler" and not enough crab. These crab cakes, however, are packed with real crab, and that's what makes them stand out. They were a favorite on the lunch menu at Three Fat Pigs, where we also served them as "Crabby Patty" burgers. Once you try these, they'll quickly become your go-to crab cakes.*

**Mix crab cakes:** In a large bowl, mix ¼ cup mayonnaise, Dijon, Worcestershire, egg and Old Bay Seasoning. Add crabmeat, breadcrumbs, parsley, lemon zest, salt, and pepper. Gently fold to combine taking care not to break up the crab too much.

**Form:** Gently shape into 6 to 8 crab cakes using ⅓ cup of crab mixture each and put on a plate in refrigerator for at least 1 hour.

**Sear:** Heat oil in a large nonstick pan over medium-high heat. Cook the crab cakes in batches for about 3 to 5 minutes on each side until golden brown.

**Make aioli:** In a separate bowl, mix 1 cup mayonnaise and wasabi paste. Mix well and serve as a dipping sauce alongside the crab cakes.

Serve the crab cakes immediately after cooking.

**Prep time:** 5 minutes
**Cook time:** 25 minutes

**SERVES 4**

# MANILA CLAMS WITH LEMONGRASS, CHILI, AND SAKE BUTTER SAUCE

- 1 tablespoon neutral oil
- 2 tablespoons minced ginger
- 1 (3-inch) piece of lemongrass, smashed
- 1 tablespoon sambal oelek
- 2 tablespoons minced garlic
- 2 tablespoons white sugar
- ¼ cup of cherry tomatoes, sliced in half
- 1 cup sake
- 3 pounds cooked Manila clams
- ½ cup butter
- 1 tablespoon chopped cilantro

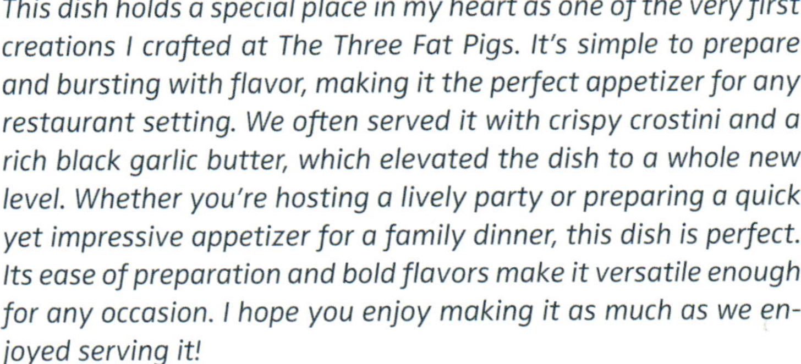

*This dish holds a special place in my heart as one of the very first creations I crafted at The Three Fat Pigs. It's simple to prepare and bursting with flavor, making it the perfect appetizer for any restaurant setting. We often served it with crispy crostini and a rich black garlic butter, which elevated the dish to a whole new level. Whether you're hosting a lively party or preparing a quick yet impressive appetizer for a family dinner, this dish is perfect. Its ease of preparation and bold flavors make it versatile enough for any occasion. I hope you enjoy making it as much as we enjoyed serving it!*

---

**Cook aromatics:** Heat oil in a saucepan over medium-high heat. Add ginger, lemongrass, and sambal and cook for 2 minutes. Add garlic, sugar, and tomatoes and cook another 2 minutes.

**Make sauce:** Pour in sake and add clams. Cook sake down by half. Turn heat to low and add butter while stirring to allow butter to melt. Once butter is melted, turn off heat and toss in cilantro.

Serve with toasted bread.

*If you are not into as much spice, you can cut the sambal in half.*

Prep time: 20 minutes
Cook time: 30 minutes

**SERVES 4**

# SHRIMP AND GRITS

1 tablespoon neutral oil
½ yellow onion, julienned
20 shrimp, peeled and deveined
2 cloves garlic, minced
1 teaspoon paprika
1 teaspoon garlic powder
Big pinch of salt (and more to taste)
½ teaspoon black pepper
½ teaspoon onion powder
½ teaspoon cayenne pepper
½ teaspoon dried oregano
¼ cup bourbon
½ cup cream
2 tablespoons butter
2 cups water
2 cups milk
1 cup grits
3 tablespoons butter

*If someone asked me to name the most popular recipes in this cookbook, this would be at the top of the list. A staple on my menu at The Three Fat Pigs, this was a top seller. The rub makes a great dry BBQ rub as well for your favorite cut of meat, and it also makes a fabulous blackening seasoning. Shrimp and Grits is nothing new, but this recipe with its touch of bourbon will become one of your favorite ways to make it.*

**Cook shrimp and aromatics:** In a pan over medium-high heat, add oil and cook onions until translucent. Add shrimp and cook until about halfway cooked, about 3 minutes. Add minced garlic and cook another 2 minutes.

**Make spice blend:** Mix all the spices together. Add spices to the shrimp and add bourbon, allowing it to cook down by at least half. Be careful if using an open flame as the bourbon will catch on fire.

**Finish shrimp:** Add cream and cook on medium-low until it starts to thicken a little. Stir in butter. Season with salt if you need more.

**Make grits:** In a pot over medium-high heat, bring water, milk, and a pinch of salt to a boil. Whisk in the grits and continue whisking until thickened and smooth. Stir in butter.

Spoon grits into a bowl and pour shrimp on top with sauce. Enjoy!

Prep time: 5 minutes
Cook time: 3 hours (to freeze)

**SERVES 4**

# ICE CAKES

½ cup sweetened condensed milk
2 tablespoons heavy whipping cream
6 ounces lemon-lime soda
12 ounces strawberry flavored soda

*I've always had a sweet tooth, and this dessert definitely helps me scratch that itch. One of Hawai'i's most popular sweet treat, the famous shave ice, is a distant cousin to the ice cake—even though ice cake is treated like the distant cousin you don't talk to often. I grew up eating this out of plastic cups with wooden flat spoons at my grandma's house every summer. It was an easy dessert that was refreshing on hot, humid Hilo summer days. My favorite part about this recipe is the versatility. You can use any flavor soda you want, creating endless options to also satisfy your and your family's sweet tooth as well.*

**Combine:** In a bowl, combine condensed milk and cream; mix well. Add the soda and lightly mix until just incorporated, leaving some air bubbles intact.

**Freeze:** Ladle the milk and soda mixture into 6-ounce plastic cups and place in freezer. Allow to freeze for at least 3 hours.

*Feel free to use any flavor soda you like instead of strawberry. They all work and make this recipe versatile. Try drizzling a little condensed milk or li hing mui powder on top for a little sweet twist.*

# COFFEE CRÈME BRÛLÉE

**Prep time:** 30 minutes
**Cook time:** 35 minutes (plus 2 hours to chill)

**SERVES 6**

- 5 large egg yolks
- 1 pinch salt
- ½ cup white sugar plus extra for caramelizing
- 2 cups heavy cream
- 1 teaspoon vanilla extract
- 2 teaspoons espresso powder
- 6 teaspoons sugar

*Crème Brûlée may seem intimidating at first, especially with the need for a torch, but once you understand the basic technique, it becomes second nature. The foundation of all crème brûlées is a custard made by slowly tempering eggs and sugar with hot cream. While coffee is a popular flavor, the possibilities are endless. You can infuse the cream with black tea, lavender, lemongrass, or any other flavor that sparks your creativity. To make a flavored crème brûlée, simply steep your chosen ingredient into the cream while heating, then strain it before tempering the egg mixture. Enjoy the process and let your imagination run wild!*

Preheat oven to 325°F.

**Make custard:** In a stainless steel bowl, whisk egg yolks, salt, and sugar together well.

In a sauce pan over medium-high heat, cook cream, vanilla, and espresso powder until it just starts to boil (do not let it boil over). Remove from heat and SLOWLY add the hot cream into the egg mixture whisking constantly as you are adding the cream. Use a spoon and remove the foam from the top of the mixture (custard base) once mixed.

**Fill ramekins:** Pour the cream and egg mixture into individual ramekins a little over halfway up. Put ramekins into a roasting pan or baking dish and pour water into pan until it is about halfway up the outside of the ramekins.

**Bake:** Gently put into oven and bake for 30 to 35 minutes until the centers are set and they have a slight wiggle in the middle. Remove from the water and allow to cool to room temperature, then cover and refrigerate until fully chilled (about 2 hours up to 3 days).

*If you don't have espresso powder, you can use coffee grounds. Just strain through a fine mesh sieve before mixing into the egg-sugar mixture.*

**Brûlée:** When ready to serve, sprinkle 2 teaspoons of sugar on top of each custard, swirling to spread evenly. Torch the top, moving in a circular pattern until the whole surface is caramelized to a deep amber color. Allow the sugar to cool a bit as it will start to harden.

Prep time: 10 minutes
Cook time: 15 minutes

**MAKES ABOUT 5 SANDWICHES**

# MAC NUT, TOFFEE, AND COCONUT ICE CREAM SANDWICH

1 cup butter, softened
1 cup brown sugar
½ cup granulated white sugar
½ tablespoon vanilla extract
1 large egg
1 large egg yolk
2½ cups all-purpose flour
½ teaspoon salt
½ teaspoon baking soda
1 cup toffee bits
¼ cup chopped macadamia nuts
¼ cup sweetened coconut flakes, toasted
Pinch sea salt
2 cups vanilla Ice cream

*Cookies are simple yet timelessly popular. The cookie is my wife's recipe. Her cookies were extremely popular at our little food boutique. At The Three Fat Pigs, we created a chef's choice ice cream sandwich. One of my favorites featured this perfectly baked cookie with creamy vanilla ice cream in the middle.*

Preheat oven to 375°F. Spray a baking sheet with cooking spray; set aside.

**Make cookie dough:** In a mixer, combine the butter, brown sugar, white sugar, vanilla, whole egg, and egg yolk and mix until smooth; set aside.

In a separate bowl, combine the flour, salt, and baking soda and mix well. Add the dry ingredients to the wet ingredients and mix until incorporated Fold in the toffee bits, macadamia nuts, and coconut flakes until evenly distributed.

**Bake cookies:** Scoop about ¼ cup of dough onto the prepared baking sheet for each cookie, leaving at least 3 inches between the cookies. Sprinkle the cookies with a pinch of sea salt. Bake for 8 to 10 minutes, or until the cookies start to get a little golden but are still soft in the center. Do not overbake. Remove from the oven and allow them to cool.

**Assemble sandwich:** Make sure your ice cream is fully frozen. Scoop ice cream onto the bottom of one cookie and press the second cookie on top.

# IPPY'S HAWAIIAN BBQ

## *Coming Full Circle*

Opening Ippy's Hawaiian BBQ was a defining moment in my life, one that marked the culmination of years of dreams, hard work, and a deep connection to my family's restaurant roots. Growing up, I always knew I wanted to be a chef. After culinary school, my mind was filled with the traditional expectations of what a chef should create and where they should cook. But having been raised in family-run restaurants, I understood something deeper: food isn't just about fine dining, it's about accessibility and community. That's why I knew my first venture had to be something that everyone could enjoy—something for the people—before I ever considered opening a sit-down restaurant.

**There were endless obstacles, from delays with the fire hydrant across the street (no water, no fire inspection) to tearing down an entire wall right after building it because we hadn't used metal framing. But through all the setbacks, there was one driving force: my desire to build something solid, something lasting.**

Looking back, I realize that life always comes full circle. We are shaped by our past, influenced by those who came before us, and inspired by their stories. A legacy isn't just a collection of events—it's the impact those moments have on the future. My father's restaurant, the Kamuela Deli, where he served traditional Hawaiian plate lunches, left a lasting impression on me and ignited the spark that eventually became my own legacy.

The first Ippy's Hawaiian BBQ opened in 2012, in a small food court in Waikoloa. It was a few months before I launched The Three Fat Pigs, my sit-down restaurant, and to say I was nervous would be an understatement. We opened right before Christmas, right when the busy season was in full swing, and I hadn't even hired a team yet. It was just me, my family and our kitchen manager, Kelvin—who had worked at Solimene's for my mom, another one of those full circle moments. The opening day was an absolute whirlwind, the kind of busy that makes you question everything: *Can I really do this every day? How do we open tomorrow if we sold out of everything today?* But, after years of watching my parents run restaurants, I knew we would push through. It was tough, no doubt, but our first location found success quickly. We were always busy, and the smiles on our customers' faces told me we were doing something right. Still, we learned fast: we needed more help if we were going to keep up with demand.

It wasn't until a few years later that I made the decision to expand. In 2018, I found the perfect location for our second Ippy's Hawaiian BBQ in Waimea—a former car dealership right in my hometown. With the majestic Waimea mountains as a backdrop, it felt like the perfect place to build something meaningful. But the space needed a lot of work. As an entrepreneur without investors backing me, I had no choice but to roll up my sleeves and get to work. The physical labor that went into transforming that space was grueling—my back and knees still feel it when I think about

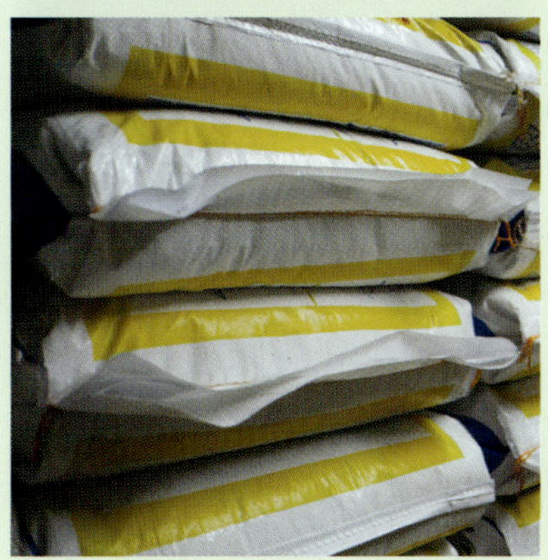

jackhammering floors to lay plumbing or calling my uncle to help lift the hoods onto the roof with a crane. It was a true family effort from day one. There were endless obstacles, from delays with the fire hydrant across the street (no water, no fire inspection) to tearing down an entire wall right after building it because we hadn't used metal framing. But through all the setbacks, there was one driving force: my desire to build something solid, something lasting. With my wife pregnant with our daughter Grace, I knew the importance of creating a future—not just for me, but for my daughters.

Opening night at Ippy's Waimea was smoother than our first location, but running a stand-alone spot brought a whole new set of challenges. The food court was one thing, but managing a full-service restaurant with its own set of responsibilities was a whole different ballgame. Then, of course, came the pandemic. Like so many others, our business was deeply affected. When travel picked up again in Waikoloa, we were slammed with customers, but we had lost so many employees and struggled to find replacements. Keeping up with the quality of food that we were known for was becoming harder, so we made the tough decision to consolidate everything at our Waimea location.

Despite the adversity, I am forever grateful for Ippy's Hawaiian BBQ—it is the heartbeat of my family's livelihood, putting food on the table and a roof over our heads. When I see my daughters running around the restaurant, laughing and playing, I'm transported back to my childhood. I remember lying on rice bags in the dry storage room while my dad ran his Hawaiian plate lunch restaurant and bringing my friends there after school to enjoy a meal. Now, I see my own daughters do the same thing I did as a child, and I realize how deeply life has come full circle. The past has shaped the present, and we're carrying it forward.

Ippy's Hawaiian BBQ is still serving the same food I grew up with—comforting, soulful Hawaiian plates—prepared

with the same recipes that have been passed down for generations. My kitchen manager, Chazon, who worked alongside my dad in his restaurant and then with my mom at her restaurant, now has his own son working with us too. It's a beautiful continuation of the legacy. Life isn't about how much you make; it's about how you make it. And above all, it's about family and community, those connections that make everything meaningful. When that circle comes back around, we want to greet it with open arms, full hearts, and no regrets.

**When I see my daughters running around the restaurant, laughing and playing, I'm transported back to my childhood.**

*» Ippy with his daughter, Poppy.*

**Prep time:** 15 minutes
**Cook time:** 5 minutes

**SERVES 4**

# SHOYU POKE

- 2 pounds fresh 'ahi, cut into 1½ inch cubes
- ½ tablespoon kosher salt
- ¼ cup Aloha Shoyu
- ¼ cup white sugar
- 1 tablespoon minced garlic
- 1 tablespoon minced ginger
- 2 teaspoons sambal oelek or sriracha
- ½ teaspoon sesame oil
- Two pieces of green onion, chopped into little rounds
- ½ avocado cut into 1-inch chunks
- Toasted sesame seeds

*For a tasty treat, use sheets of nori and scoop up the poke with a little rice, making little poke sushi snacks.*

*While not the traditional Hawaiian-style poke, shoyu poke is arguably the most popular style of poke in Hawai'i. The word "poke" means to cut or slice crosswise into pieces, which is a fitting description since poke typically refers to cubed raw fish, in this case, 'ahi. I demonstrate this recipe every week during my "Poke and Sashimi Master Class," and trust me, if some of the people I teach can make it, you can definitely do it too. Growing up, this is the dish my dad always prepared for us to take to the beach, and I usually enjoy it with crispy fried wonton chips or Maui onion chips.*

**Prepare 'ahi:** Place the 'ahi in a colander and sprinkle with kosher salt. Let it rest for about 15 minutes to allow excess liquid to drain from the fish.

**Make sauce:** In a mixing bowl, whisk together the Aloha Shoyu, sugar, garlic, ginger, sambal, and sesame oil until fully combined.

**Mix fish:** After the 'ahi has released its liquid, transfer it into the prepared sauce and gently toss to coat. Carefully fold in the green onions and avocado, ensuring even distribution without mashing the avocado.

Garnish with toasted sesame seeds and serve over a bed of hot rice, at the beach, or with crispy wonton chips—my personal favorite!

Prep time: 30 minutes
Cook time: none

**SERVES 4**

# SPICY 'AHI POKE

2 pounds fresh 'ahi, cut into 1-inch cubes
½ tablespoon kosher salt
½ cup mayonnaise
3 tablespoons sriracha
1 tablespoon mirin
1 teaspoon sesame oil
1 tablespoon minced ginger
1 avocado, cut into 1-inch chunks (optional)
2 pieces scallions, cut into ¼-inch rounds
Sprinkle of furikake

*This sauce is incredibly versatile and can elevate countless dishes. Use it to blend scraped 'ahi into spicy tuna rolls, mix it with crabmeat for California rolls, or even drizzle it as a spicy mayo on sandwiches for an extra kick. Its adaptability makes it a staple in many kitchens, especially here in Hawai'i. Spicy 'ahi is so popular on the islands that you'll always find it as an option at local grocery stores, a testament to its status as a go-to comfort food. For my family, it was more than just a side dish—it was a tradition. We'd pack up spicy 'ahi, a fresh batch of this sauce, and a pack of dried nori for beach or picnic days. Scooping the creamy, flavorful 'ahi onto crisp nori sheets while sitting on the sand was the perfect way to enjoy our family excursions.*

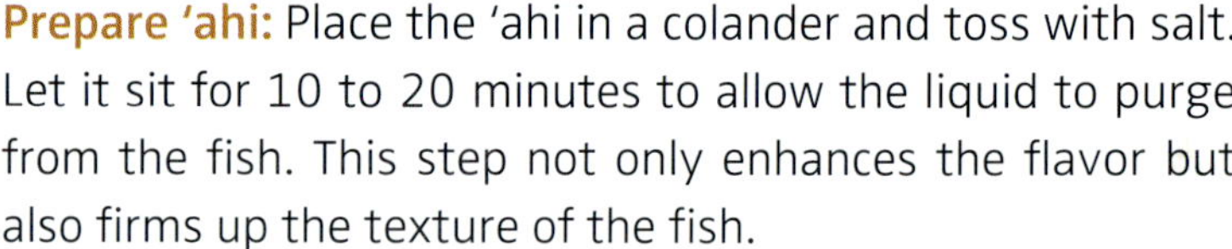

**Prepare 'ahi:** Place the 'ahi in a colander and toss with salt. Let it sit for 10 to 20 minutes to allow the liquid to purge from the fish. This step not only enhances the flavor but also firms up the texture of the fish.

**Mix sauce:** In a mixing bowl, combine the mayonnaise, sriracha, mirin, sesame oil, and ginger. Stir until well-blended.

Add the 'ahi, scallions, avocado, and furikake to the bowl, and gently toss to coat the fish in the sauce.

Serve over hot rice or enjoy on its own.

Prep time: 20 minutes
Cook time: 30 minutes

SERVES 4

# ASIAN CHICKEN SALAD

- 1 cup hot water
- 3/4 cup sugar
- 1/4 cup distilled white vinegar
- Pinch of salt
- 3 cloves garlic, minced
- 1/2 teaspoon fish sauce (patis) (about one dash)
- 8 sheets of wonton wrapper cut into 1/4-inch wide strips
- 2 heads iceberg lettuce (or mixed greens)
- 2 pieces Chicken Katsu (page 130)
- Dressing to taste (some like more some like less)
- 5 tablespoons chopped roasted peanuts
- 2 mandarin oranges, supremed

*This salad has earned its place as one of the most popular dishes at Ippy's Hawaiian BBQ, but its story begins at my dad's iconic Hawaiian restaurant, the Kamuela Deli. If you're searching for a light and healthy salad, this might not fit the bill—but if bold flavors and irresistible textures are what you're after, you've found the perfect dish. The magic lies in the dressing. Sweet yet balanced with just enough garlic to give it a gentle kick, it coats the greens beautifully without being overpowering. Unlike thick, emulsified vinaigrettes, this dressing has a light, pourable consistency, so it's best to toss it with the greens before serving to ensure every bite bursts with flavor. At the Kamuela Deli, the salad was traditionally topped with crispy bean thread noodles, which added the perfect crunch. While those have become harder to find over the years, I've found that crispy wonton strips make an excellent substitute, preserving the texture that makes this salad so special. Once you try it, you will see why it's a fan favorite. This salad isn't just a dish, it's a delicious tribute to the flavors and traditions that shaped my culinary journey.*

**Make dressing:** In a pot, bring water to a boil, then turn off the heat. Add the sugar and stir until fully dissolved. Add the vinegar, salt, garlic, and fish sauce to the pot. Stir to combine. (This dressing can be stored in the refrigerator for up to 2 weeks.)

**Fry wonton strips:** Heat a small pot of oil to 350°F (175°C). Fry the wonton strips in batches until they are golden brown and crispy. Remove and drain on paper towels.

*To supreme the orange, carefully cut and separate the segments while removing the skin, pith, membranes, and seeds. If you can't find fresh mandarin oranges you can use regular oranges or even the canned mandarin oranges work as well.*

**Make salad:** Chop the lettuce into bite-sized pieces and place it in a large bowl. Cut the chicken into small, ½-inch cubes or slices. Add a few tablespoons of the dressing to the lettuce and toss to coat. Add more dressing to taste, as desired.

Top the salad with peanuts, orange supremes, chicken, and crispy wonton strips. Serve immediately.

**Prep time:** 20 minutes
**Cook time:** 1 hour

**SERVES 4**

# CHICKEN PAPAYA SOUP

2 tablespoons neutral oil
2 pounds boneless skinless chicken thigh, cut into bite-size cubes
1 yellow onion, diced
1 (2-inch) piece of ginger, minced
3½ cups chicken broth
2 cups water
2 tablespoons patis
5 cloves garlic, minced
2 tablespoons Aloha Shoyu
1 green papaya, cut in 2-inch cubes (see note)
1 tablespoon minced cilantro
Salt and pepper to taste

*If you can't find green papaya you can use pipinola (chayote) or a squash of your choice, just cook accordingly. In Hawai'i we also use malunggay (moringa) leaves. If using, add with the green papaya.*

*Growing up, there was a field full of pipinola (chayote) right across the street from my house. My mom would often use this versatile ingredient in her cooking, swapping it for green papaya in her soup. Pipinola and green papaya have a texture similar to potato but with far less starch, making it light yet satisfying—a true hidden gem of an ingredient. To me, this Filipino soup is the ultimate comfort food, perfect for those chilly Waimea nights or whenever you need something to warm both body and soul. It's a dish that not only fills the stomach but also brings a sense of nostalgia and home with every spoonful.*

**Cook chicken:** In a large pot, heat oil over medium-high heat. Add the chicken and cook, turning occasionally, until browned on all sides. Add the onion and ginger to the pot, sautéing for about 3 minutes until the onions are translucent and fragrant.

**Make soup:** Pour in the chicken broth, water, patis, minced garlic, and Aloha Shoyu. Bring the mixture to a simmer, then cover and cook for 30 minutes, or until the chicken is fork-tender. Add the papaya to the pot, cover, and cook for an additional 20 minutes, or until the green papaya becomes tender. Stir in fresh cilantro and adjust the seasoning to taste. Serve hot.

Prep time: 25 minutes (overnight for rice)
Cook time: 30 minutes

**SERVES 4**

# LOCAL-STYLE KIMCHEE FRIED RICE

*Fried rice is a beloved dish throughout the Pacific, with every region adding its own twist. At Ippy's Hawaiian BBQ, we make our fried rice from scratch, often preparing a large batch at the start of service to keep things fresh and fast. Guests can swap out regular rice for our signature fried rice in any plate they order, making it a versatile and tasty option. While I've kept this recipe simple, in Hawai'i, fried rice is often made with Spam and kamaboko (fish cake), which adds a unique flavor. Think of this recipe as a canvas—add your favorite ingredients to truly make it your own.*

- 1 tablespoon neutral oil
- ½ yellow onion, minced
- ½ red bell pepper, diced
- ½ cup chopped scallions, white and green parts
- 1 cup kimchee, cut into strips
- 3 cloves garlic, minced
- 2 teaspoons sesame oil
- 3 cups cooked rice, chilled overnight
- 2 tablespoons Aloha Shoyu
- 1 tablespoon oyster sauce (optional)
- 1 teaspoon Worcestershire sauce
- 1 tablespoon hoisin sauce
- 1 large egg, beaten
- Salt and pepper to taste

**Sauté vegetables:** In a wok or large nonstick sauté pan, heat oil over medium-high heat. Add the onions and cook for about 3 minutes, or until they become translucent. Add the bell pepper, scallions, and kimchee. Continue cooking for another 3 minutes, stirring constantly.

**Stir-fry rice:** Stir in the garlic and sesame oil, then quickly add the rice. Use a wooden spoon or spatula to break up any clumps of rice. Pour in the Aloha Shoyu, oyster sauce, Worcestershire sauce, and hoisin sauce. Cook over medium heat for another 5 minutes, stirring occasionally to allow the rice to absorb the sauces.

Once the liquid is fully absorbed and the rice is hot, create a well in the center of the rice, exposing the bottom of the pan. Add the beaten egg into the well and let it cook for about 2 minutes. Stir the egg into the rice, allowing the hot rice to scramble it. Once the egg is cooked through, season with salt and pepper to taste. Serve immediately.

*Placing the rice in the refrigerator overnight is very necessary as fresh hot sticky rice doesn't absorb the liquid properly and will create a sticky mess, so don't skip this step!*

*» Ippy interviewing Li'a Vicente, a kalo farmer in Waipi'o, on his television show* Eating Our Roots.

# CHICKEN KATSU

**Prep time:** 30 minutes (or 24 hours if marinating)
**Cook time:** 45 minutes

**SERVES 4**

½ cup ketchup
4 tablespoons Worcestershire sauce
2 tablespoons oyster sauce
1 tablespoon brown sugar
2 teaspoons black pepper
2 teaspoons salt
1 teaspoon black pepper
1 teaspoon white pepper
2 teaspoons garlic powder
1½ teaspoons sesame oil
3 large eggs, beaten
2 tablespoons shao xing cooking wine (optional, can substitute dry sherry)
3 tablespoons cornstarch
4 pounds boneless, skinless chicken thighs
Neutral oil for frying
3 cups panko bread crumbs
4 cups cooked white rice, for serving

*You can make this a few days ahead of time if you want, just freeze the chicken after you bread it and allow it to thaw out before frying it. This would allow you to make a big batch days before you need it.*

*Fried chicken is undeniably one of the most beloved dishes in the world, celebrated in countless variations—from classic buttermilk fried chicken to Korean-style wings and crispy tenders. For me, though, nothing compares to chicken katsu. What sets chicken katsu apart is the use of juicy, marinated chicken thighs, which ensure every bite is incredibly moist and packed with flavor. Coated in light, crispy panko and deboned for easy eating, it's a dish that's as satisfying as it is simple. My first kitchen experience was manning the fryer station at my dad's Hawaiian restaurant, and I can still vividly remember the joy of cooking chicken katsu. It was a customer favorite then, and it remains one of the most popular dishes at my own Hawaiian restaurant today—and with good reason. Chicken katsu isn't just comfort food; it's a connection to my roots and a celebration of timeless flavor.*

---

**Prepare sauce:** In a mixing bowl, combine ketchup, Worcestershire sauce, oyster sauce, brown sugar, and black pepper. Stir well until the mixture is smooth and fully incorporated.

**Make marinade:** In a separate bowl, mix together salt, black pepper, white pepper, garlic powder, sesame oil, eggs, cooking wine, and cornstarch. Coat the chicken thighs in the mixture, then let them marinate for at least 2 hours, or preferably overnight.

**Cook chicken:** Fill a pot with enough oil to submerge the chicken. Heat the oil to 350°F (175°C).

Place the panko breadcrumbs in a shallow bowl or large plate. Before breading, give the chicken mixture a quick stir to ensure the cornstarch hasn't settled at the bottom. One piece at a time, dredge each chicken thigh in the panko breadcrumbs, pressing lightly to coat. Carefully add the chicken to the hot oil and fry until golden brown and crispy, or until the chicken reaches an internal temperature of 165°F (74°C).

Serve with white rice.

# CHICKEN LONG RICE

Prep time: 1 hour
Cook time: 1 hour

**SERVES 4**

- 5 dried shiitake mushrooms
- 3 cups water
- 7 ounces bean thread noodles (saifun)
- ½ yellow onion
- 3 tablespoons neutral oil
- 4 boneless skinless chicken thighs, cut into 1-inch pieces
- 1 (3-inch) piece fresh ginger, lightly smashed
- 4 cups chicken broth
- 1 teaspoon salt
- ½ carrot, julienned
- 3 scallions, both green and white parts, cut into 2-inch pieces

*My dad's trick with this dish is blending the onion before using them, this allows it to melt into the dish creating optimum flavor.*

*What I love most about this dish is the rich, warming ginger flavor infused into the broth—it's the heart and soul of every bite. At local gatherings, chicken long rice is an absolute staple, a dish you'll always find on the table. For me, my dad's version has always been the gold standard. I might be a little biased, but there's something about the way he makes it that stands out, with just the right balance of savory broth and tender chicken. It's the kind of comfort food that brings people together and reminds me of home.*

**Prepare mushrooms:** In a small bowl, combine the dried mushrooms with 3 cups of water. Let them soak for 1 hour. Afterward, remove the mushrooms, reserving 1 cup of the soaking liquid. Slice the mushrooms lengthwise into strips, discarding the stems. Set the mushrooms aside.

**Soak noodles:** In another bowl, soak the noodles for 30 minutes to rehydrate and soften. Drain and set aside.

**Cook chicken:** In a food processor, purée the onion until smooth; set aside.

In a large pot, heat oil over medium-high heat. Add the chicken and cook until lightly browned on all sides. Add the pureed onions to the pot and sauté for another 2 minutes, until fragrant. Add the sliced mushrooms, reserved mushroom soaking liquid, ginger, chicken broth, and salt to the pot. Bring to a simmer and cook for about 20 minutes, or until the chicken is fully cooked.

**Add noodles and carrots:** Stir in the noodles and carrot, then continue to simmer for another 20 minutes until the noodles are plump, translucent, and tender, and the chicken is fork-tender.

Garnish with scallions and serve. For the best noodle absorption, let the dish sit for about 30 minutes before eating, as the noodles will continue to soak up the broth until hardly any is left.

*Ippy interviewing Earl Yamamoto of B.E.S.T. Farms in Waimea on his television show* Eating Our Roots.

Prep time: 20 minutes, plus 3 hours to marinate
Cook time: 30 minutes

**SERVES 4**

5 large eggs
2 tablespoons sake
2 teaspoons salt
2 teaspoons garlic powder
1 teaspoon black pepper
2¾ cups cornstarch, divided use
4 pounds boneless, skin-on chicken thighs
Neutral oil for frying
1½ cups all-purpose flour
2 cups water
½ cup distilled white vinegar
1 cup sugar
½ teaspoon salt
1 to 2 drops yellow food coloring (optional)
1 teaspoon lemon extract (see note)
5 lemon slices
1 tablespoon cornstarch
2 tablespoons water

*If you can't find lemon extract, you can use the zest of 2 lemons instead.*

# LEMON CHICKEN

*This dish is a perfect representation of the melting pot that is Hawai'i—a place where diverse cultures come together to create something truly unique. Rooted in Chinese culinary traditions, it has become a beloved favorite here in the islands, reflecting both its origins and the local flavors that make Hawai'i's cuisine so special. The dish combines the iconic sweet-and-sour flavors of Chinese cooking with a light, crispy coating that gives each bite a satisfying crunch. The balance of tangy and sweet notes is brightened by a subtle tropical flair. This culinary fusion is more than just a meal—it's a celebration of Hawai'i's multicultural heritage, showcasing how different traditions can come together to create something truly unforgettable.*

**Prepare chicken:** In a mixing bowl, combine the eggs, sake, salt, garlic powder, pepper, and ¾ cup of cornstarch. Whisk until smooth. Add the chicken and stir to coat. Cover and refrigerate for at least 3 hours to marinate.

**Fry chicken:** In a large pot, pour enough oil (about 2 inches) to fully submerge the chicken. Heat the oil to 375°F.

In a separate bowl, combine the flour and the remaining 2 cups of cornstarch. Dredge each piece of chicken in the flour mixture, ensuring a thick, even coating. Carefully add the coated chicken to the hot oil, frying for about 8 minutes, or until golden brown and crispy. The chicken is fully cooked when it reaches an internal temperature of 165°F. If necessary, cook the chicken in batches to avoid overcrowding. Once cooked, transfer the fried chicken to a paper towel-lined plate to drain any excess oil.

**Prepare sauce:** In a small saucepan, combine water, vinegar, sugar, salt, food coloring (if using), lemon extract, and lemon slices. Bring the mixture to a simmer over medium heat.

In a small bowl, mix cornstarch and water to create a slurry. Slowly add this mixture to the simmering sauce, stirring constantly until the sauce thickens to a consistency that coats the back of a spoon.

Cut the fried chicken into strips and pour the sauce over the top. Serve immediately.

Prep time: 15 minutes
Cook time: 20 minutes

**SERVES 4**

# BEEF AND EGGPLANT STIR-FRY

3 tablespoons neutral flavored oil, divided use
1½ pounds ground beef
1 eggplant, cut into 1-inch cubes
1 large mild chili, sliced in rounds (like a hatch chili or poblano)
2 Hawaiian chili peppers (can use bird's eye chilies or 2 teaspoons red pepper flakes)
5 cloves garlic, minced
2 tablespoons fish sauce (patis)
4 tablespoons oyster sauce
1 tablespoon hoisin sauce
Pinch of white sugar
1 handful Thai basil leaves (about 1 cup)

*If you arent a spicy food lover, you can adjust the chili to your liking.*

*This is one of my go-to dishes whenever I'm cooking for my family at home—it's always at the top of my wife's request list because it's one of her all-time favorites. It's easy to see why: the depth of umami in this recipe is perfect, creating layers of savory flavor that are both comforting and satisfying. What I love most is that it's a one-pot wonder—simple to prepare, easy to clean up, and packed with bold, rich flavors that make it feel like much more than the sum of its parts. Served over a bowl of hot, steamed rice, this dish is pure comfort food and the kind of meal that brings everyone to the table with a smile. Trust me, once you make it, this will quickly become your family's favorite go-to dish as well—a recipe you'll find yourself coming back to time and again for its simplicity, heartiness, and unbeatable flavor.*

**Brown beef:** In a pan over medium-high heat, add 1 tablespoon of oil. Brown the beef, then set it aside.

**Cook vegetables:** Add 2 tablespoons of oil to the pan, then toss in the eggplant and chilies. Sauté for about 5 minutes, or until the eggplant is soft and cooked through. Add the garlic and cook for an additional 2 minutes, making sure not to burn the garlic, and add browned beef back in.

**Combine sauces:** Stir in the fish sauce, oyster sauce, hoisin sauce, and sugar. Cook everything together for another 5 minutes, allowing the flavors to meld.

Toss in fresh Thai basil and serve the dish hot over rice or with a fresh salad.

Prep time: 1 hour
Cook time: 35 minutes

**SERVES 4**

# BEEF TOMATO

*At Ippy's Hawaiian BBQ, our Beef Tomato special is a true Hawaiian classic. While we typically use teriyaki beef at the restaurant, here we've chosen to marinate one of my personal favorite cuts—flank steak—for a unique twist to this dish. What I love most about Beef Tomato is how its name changes across the island. In most places, it's called Beef Tomato, but over in Hilo, they call it Tomato Beef. Hilo marches to the beat of its own drum, and I'm all for it!*

ALOHA SHOYU COMPANY

1 pound flank steak, sliced into strips against the grain
2 tablespoons neutral oil, divided use
½ yellow onion, julienned
1 celery stalk, sliced thin against the grain
1 green bell pepper
2 tomatoes, sliced into 8 wedges each
3 green onions, cut into 2-inch pieces
Salt and pepper to taste
3 cloves garlic, minced
2 tablespoons Aloha Shoyu
1 teaspoon sesame oil
1 tablespoon hoisin sauce
2 tablespoons oyster sauce
3 tablespoons water
1 tablespoon white sugar
1 tablespoon rice vinegar
1 tablespoon cornstarch
1 tablespoon Aloha Shoyu

**Marinate meat:** In a bowl, combine all the marinade ingredients: garlic, 2 tablespoons of Aloha Shoyu, sesame oil, and hoisin. Add the meat, tossing to coat. Let it marinate for at least an hour.

**Brown meat:** Heat 1 tablespoon of oil in a pan over medium-high heat. Once hot, add the marinated meat and cook, turning occasionally, until browned on all sides. Remove meat and set aside.

**Sauté vegetables:** In the same pan, add 1 tablespoon of oil. Sauté the onions and celery for about 3 minutes. Add the bell pepper and cook for another 2 minutes, until slightly tender.

Return the browned meat to the pan. Add the tomatoes. Cook for about 5 minutes, allowing the tomatoes to soften and begin to break down.

**Mix sauce:** Mix all the ingredients for the sauce in a bowl: oyster sauce, water, sugar, rice vinegar, cornstarch, and 1 tablespoon Aloha Shoyu; mix well as cornstarch will settle at bottom. Stir sauce into meat mixture, then reduce the heat to medium. Allow the sauce to simmer until it thickens and coats the meat and vegetables. Toss in green onions, season to taste, and serve over rice.

*When cutting the flank steak, it is very important to cut against the grain. This will create a much more tender bite.*

Prep time: 2 hours to 24 hours
Cook time: 30 minutes

SERVES 4

# GRILLED KOREAN KALBI SHORT RIBS

- 2 full pieces of green onion
- 1 tablespoon toasted sesame seeds
- 3 tablespoons water
- ¼ cup Aloha Shoyu
- ¼ cup water
- ¼ cup white sugar
- 2 teaspoons sesame oil
- 1 tablespoon sambal (can substitute sriracha)
- 12 pieces of short ribs, cut a little over ½-inch thick against the bone, usually has 3 bones (could substitute a steak if you can't find short ribs)
- 2 yellow or sweet onion, cut into ½-inch cubes
- ½ carrot, cut into ¼-inch thick sticks
- 1 bell pepper, cut into ½-inch sticks
- 1 clove garlic, crushed
- 2 teaspoons chili pepper flakes
- 1½ cups water
- 1½ cups distilled white vinegar
- ½ cup white sugar
- 1 teaspoon salt

*Kalbi short ribs are, without a doubt, one of the most flavorful cuts of meat you'll ever taste. The sweet and salty marinade doesn't just coat the surface—it seeps deep into the meat, creating layers of flavor that caramelize beautifully on a hot grill or sizzling pan. The result? Tender, smoky, and utterly irresistible. Whenever we visit my wife's family on the mainland, this is the one dish they always request. It's become a family favorite, and for good reason. I've often dreamed of packaging and selling these ribs in grocery stores, because I truly believe they're one of the most perfect cuts of meat out there. Growing up, kalbi wasn't something we ate often—it was considered a luxury, too expensive for regular meals. But now, with my own restaurant, I make the most of every opportunity to enjoy it. Kalbi short ribs have become a celebration of flavor and a reminder of how far I've come.*

---

**Prepare marinade:** In a food processor, combine green onions, toasted sesame seeds, and 3 tablespoons of water. Blend until well-minced.

In a pot over medium-high heat, add Aloha Shoyu, ¼ cup of water, sugar, sesame oil, sambal, and the green onion mixture. Cook until the sugar has dissolved, then remove from heat and allow to cool.

Marinate the kalbi for at least 2 hours, but preferably overnight, for the best flavor.

**Make pickled vegetables:** Place the onions, carrots, bell pepper, garlic, and chili flakes in a glass jar. In a saucepan, combine water, vinegar, sugar, and salt. Bring to a boil over

high heat. Once boiling, turn off the heat and pour the hot brine over the vegetables in the jar. Set aside to cool. Seal the jar and refrigerate for at least 24 hours before serving. The pickled vegetables will keep in the refrigerator for up to 3 weeks.

**Cook kalbi:** Preheat the grill to high. Grill the kalbi for about 5 minutes on each side, allowing the sugars to caramelize. If you don't have a grill, a hot sauté pan will work as well.

Serve the kalbi with the pickled onions on the side.

*Ippy interviewing Zanga Schutte of Z-Bar Ranch in Kamuela on his television show* Eating Our Roots.

Prep time: 15 minutes
Cook time: 1 hour

**SERVES 4**

# PORK ADOBO

- 2 tablespoons neutral oil
- 2½ pounds pork butt, cut into 1½-inch cubes
- 1 tablespoon Dijon mustard
- 4 cloves garlic, minced
- 1 cup water
- 1 cup coconut milk
- 1 cup vinegar (apple vinegar, sugar cane vinegar, or white vinegar will work)
- ½ cup Aloha Shoyu
- 1 teaspoon whole black peppercorn
- 3 bay leaves
- 1 tablespoon brown sugar
- 1 scallion, green parts only, cut diagonally

*Pork Adobo is a quintessential Filipino dish, and in Hawai'i's restaurant industry where Filipinos often run the kitchen, it's practically a rite of passage to encounter its bold flavors. Growing up, we worked with an older lady named Sally—though we all affectionately called her Nana Sally. She would often prepare adobo as a special, and it was always one of my favorite dishes. Using her base recipe as inspiration, I decided to create my own twist on this beloved classic. Now, a bit of advice: if you're ever around a Filipino, never claim to have the best adobo—it's a surefire way to start a debate. Everyone knows their mom or grandma makes the best, and as the rule goes, you don't mess with mom or grandma. That said, my version of adobo has its own charm, thanks to the creaminess of coconut milk and the tangy complexity of Dijon mustard. I still remember the time I made this dish on a local cooking show. Behind the scenes, I could hear whispers of doubt—adding coconut milk and mustard to adobo? It was practically heresy. But once they tasted it, the skepticism melted away. They wouldn't admit it outright, but the looks on their faces told me everything: my adobo could hold its own, even against grandma's.*

---

**Brown pork:** In a large pot, heat oil over medium-high heat and cook the pork for about 5 minutes, or until it's nicely browned on all sides.

**Make adobo:** Stir in the Dijon mustard and garlic, cooking for another 2 minutes until fragrant and the garlic softens. Add the water, coconut milk, vinegar, Aloha Shoyu, peppercorns, and bay leaves. Bring the mixture to a simmer, then cover and cook for 45 minutes.

After 45 minutes, uncover the pot and continue simmering gently, allowing the gravy to thicken. Be patient—it's worth taking your time for the best results. When the gravy reaches your desired thickness (about 25 to 30 minutes), stir in the brown sugar and cook until it's completely dissolved into the sauce.

Remove and discard the bay leaves, then garnish with scallions before serving over hot rice.

Prep time: 24 hours
Cook time: 2 hours

SERVES 6

# PORK BELLY TINONO

*Tinono is a mouthwatering crispy pork belly dish, perfectly balanced with a vibrant mix of acid and salt. It starts with lechon (a classic Filipino crispy pork dish), then is tossed with fresh tomato and onion. I first tried this dish when I was young, at Chazon's house (the Filipino chef who now runs my kitchen), and I've been hooked ever since. What began as a special at Ippy's Hawaiian BBQ quickly became a fan favorite, earning a permanent spot on our menu due to its incredible flavor and popularity. While the process is time-consuming and meticulous, the results are absolutely worth it—there's nothing quite like it. I hope that the first time you try this dish, you enjoy it as much as I did when Tata Chazon first cooked it for me at his house.*

FOR BOILING

1½ quarts water
5 cloves garlic, smashed
3 bay leaves
1 tablespoon peppercorns
3 tablespoons plus 1 teaspoon kosher salt
1 tablespoon Aloha Shoyu
3-pound slab of pork belly with skin on

FOR SPICE RUB

1 tablespoon Chinese five-spice powder
2 teaspoons black pepper
2 teaspoons granulated garlic
2 teaspoons kosher salt
1 tablespoon brown sugar

FOR THE SAUCE

2 cloves garlic, minced
2 teaspoons sambal oelek (or 2 bird chilies, finely chopped)
¼ cup of lime juice
¼ cup Aloha Shoyu
1 tablespoon water
2 teaspoons fresh ground black pepper

Neutral oil for frying
2 tomatoes, seeds cut out and sliced into ½-inch thin strips

**Prepare pork belly:** In a large pot, bring water, smashed garlic cloves, bay leaves, peppercorns, salt, and Aloha Shoyu to a boil. Once boiling, carefully add the pork belly, placing it skin side down. Reduce the heat to medium and simmer for about 60 minutes, allowing the flavors to infuse and the pork belly to tenderize.

After simmering, carefully remove the pork belly from the pot and transfer it to a wire rack to allow moisture to escape (with a pan underneath to catch any drippings) or a plate lined with paper towels to cool. Once the pork belly is cool enough to handle, mix all the ingredients for the spice rub in a bowl.

Season the meat side generously with the rub, being careful not to get any seasoning on the skin. Place the pork belly, skin side up, uncovered, in the refrigerator overnight. This crucial step allows the skin to dry out, which is key to achieving a crisp, crackling texture. Remember, moisture is the enemy of crispy pork skin.

- ¼ sweet onion, julienned (can use red onion or yellow onion instead)
- 1 teaspoon toasted sesame seeds (optional)
- 2 stalks green onion, sliced into thin rounds, white and green parts

*The sauce makes a delicious salad dressing or a sauce for sashimi. It is extremely versatile.*

**Make sauce:** To prepare the sauce, combine minced garlic, sambal oelek, lime juice, Aloha Shoyu, water, and freshly ground black pepper in a bowl. Stir until the ingredients are well incorporated, creating a flavorful balance of spice, acidity, and savory depth. This sauce can be made in advance and stored in an airtight container in the refrigerator for up to 3 weeks, making it a versatile addition to various dishes.

**Cook pork belly:** To finish the pork belly, heat oil in a large pot or deep fryer, filling it halfway. Heat the oil to 350°F, ensuring it's hot enough to crisp the skin. Carefully lower the pork belly into the oil, taking care to submerge it fully (you may choose to cut the pork belly in half to make it easier to handle). Fry until the skin turns golden brown and crispy, and the internal temperature reaches at least 165°F, indicating the pork is fully cooked. If necessary, ladle hot oil over the top of the pork belly to ensure even crisping.

Once the pork belly is crispy, remove it from the oil and let it drain on a paper towels or a wire rack. Allow it to cool slightly before cutting it into 1½-inch x 2-inch chunks.

**Finish:** In a large mixing bowl, combine the pork belly with sliced tomatoes, thinly sliced sweet onions, sesame seeds, and freshly sliced green onions. Pour the prepared sauce over the pork belly and toss everything together, ensuring each piece is evenly coated in the tangy, acidic sauce.

Create a base of steaming hot rice or a crisp, refreshing salad. Spoon the flavorful pork belly mixture over the top, garnishing with extra sesame seeds or green onions, if desired. This dish offers the perfect balance of rich, crispy pork and vibrant, zesty sauce guaranteed to make your taste buds happy.

Prep time: 20 minutes
Cook time: 45 minutes

**SERVES 4**

# PORK AND PUMPKIN

- 2 tablespoons neutral oil
- 2 pounds pork shoulder, cut into 2-inch chunks
- ½ yellow onion, diced
- 5 cloves garlic, minced
- 2 tomatoes, quartered
- 2 cups chicken broth (can use water)
- 1 tablespoon fish sauce (patis)
- 1 kabocha, peeled, seeded and cut into 2-inch chunks

*In this recipe, I use kabocha pumpkin, but butternut squash would work just as well.*

*Pork and pumpkin is a hearty, comforting one-pot dish inspired by Filipino cuisine. I learned this recipe from Uncle Ryan who has been with us at Ippy's Hawaiian BBQ for years. The natural sweetness of the pumpkin is perfectly balanced by the savory depth of fish sauce, while the tomatoes cook down to create a rich, stew-like consistency. This is comfort in a pot!*

**Cook pork:** In a pot, heat oil over medium-high heat. Add the pork and cook until browned. Add the onions and garlic and cook for another 5 minutes. Stir in the tomatoes and cook for an additional 10 minutes, allowing them to break down. Add the chicken broth and 1 tablespoon of fish sauce. Bring to a simmer, cover, and cook for 15 minutes.

**Finish:** Add the pumpkin, cover, and continue to cook until the pumpkin is soft and the pork is fork-tender.

Serve over rice and enjoy!

**Prep time:** 30 minutes
**Cook time:** 45 minutes

**SERVES 4**

# MAHI MAHI WITH CHINESE GINGER SAUCE

- ¾ cup of canola oil
- 5 tablespoons minced ginger
- 1 teaspoon ground ginger powder
- 1 teaspoon salt
- ½ teaspoon white pepper
- ¼ cup cut green onion, green and white parts
- 8 (about 4 ounce) pieces of mahi mahi fillets
- Salt and pepper for seasoning

*I've used this sauce in multiple cooking competitions on Food Network, and it's always a crowd-pleaser! It was also the very first dish I made on my YouTube cooking channel when my oldest daughter was just a baby. We proudly feature it on the menu at Ippy's Hawaiian BBQ, where it's an option for all of our fish dishes. Originally created for cold ginger chicken, I'll admit it's not my top choice for that dish, as you'll see in this recipe I love using it on seafood. The best part? You can prepare it in advance and store it in your fridge for up to three weeks, ensuring you always have some ready to go. Trust me, you'll thank me later!*

**Prepare sauce:** Heat oil in a pot until it reaches 350°F.

In a heat-resistant mixing bowl or another pot, combine fresh ginger, ginger powder, salt, and white pepper. Slowly drizzle the hot oil over the mixture, adding a little at a time. Be cautious and ensure there's enough space in the bowl or pot, as the oil will bubble up when poured. Once the bubbling subsides, stir in the green onions and allow the mixture to cool. Refrigerate until chilled, then serve cold.

**Cook mahi mahi:** Preheat a grill or sauté pan. Season the mahi generously with salt and pepper, then cook for 2 to 3 minutes on each side until the fish is fully cooked through.

Pour the chilled ginger sauce over the cooked fish and serve with hot rice or a fresh salad. The sauce also makes a delicious dressing!

*If you don't have a thermometer for your oil, you can add a whole peeled garlic clove and when the garlic clove floats and starts bubbling around the edges while turning a little brown, the oil is hot enough and you can remove the garlic.*

Prep time: 24 hours (for marinating)
Cook time: 20 minutes

SERVES 4

# HIBACHI SALMON WITH NAMASU PICKLES

- 2 Japanese cucumbers, sliced into ¼-inch rounds
- 1 carrot, julienned into ⅛ x 3-inch pieces
- ½ cup rice vinegar
- ⅓ cup water
- ⅓ cup white sugar
- 1 teaspoon salt
- 1 (¼-inch) piece of fresh ginger (optional)
- ½ teaspoon toasted sesame seeds
- ¼ cup Aloha Shoyu
- ¼ cup water
- ¼ cup white sugar
- 1 tablespoon minced garlic
- 2 tablespoons minced ginger
- 2 tablespoons sesame oil
- 3 tablespoons water
- 2 tablespoons cornstarch
- 4 salmon fillets
- Salt and pepper to taste

*Hibachi, which translates to "fire bowl" in Japanese, originally referred to ceramic bowls with grates designed for grilling meats and vegetables. Growing up, my parents often took us to Hāpuna Beach State Park, a local favorite known for its sprawling sandy shores and towering stone hibachis stationed in front of every pavilion. My dad would haul a bag of charcoal, toss it into the hibachi, light it up, and get to work cooking us incredible meals right there on the beach. He had a knack for grilling just about anything, but my favorite was always his hibachi salmon. The fish, simply grilled to perfection, was brushed with a glossy, slightly sweet teriyaki glaze that caramelized beautifully over the hot coals. He always paired it with a side of tangy pickled vegetables—sometimes crisp takuan, other times delicate pickled onions or the refreshing crunch of namasu. Those meals were simple yet unforgettable, their flavors etched into my memory as a perfect blend of the ocean breeze, crackling charcoal, and the comfort of family gatherings.*

**Prepare namasu:** Place the cucumber and carrots into a glass jar or container.

In a saucepan, combine vinegar, ⅓ cup of water, sugar, salt, and ginger. Heat over medium-high heat, stirring until the sugar and salt dissolve. Pour the brine over the cucumber and carrots, then add the sesame seeds. Set aside to cool.

Seal the container and refrigerate for at least 24 hours before serving. The namasu will stay fresh in the fridge for up to 2 weeks.

**Prepare sauce:** In a saucepan over medium-high heat, combine Aloha Shoyu, ¼ cup of water, sugar, garlic, ginger, and sesame oil. Bring to a boil until the sugar dissolves. In a small bowl, mix 3 tablespoons of water and cornstarch until fully dissolved. Gradually add the cornstarch mixture into the boiling sauce, stirring until it thickens.

**Prepare salmon:** Preheat a grill to high heat and lightly spray with cooking spray. Season the salmon with salt and pepper. If the salmon has skin, start by cooking it skin-side down. Cook for about 5 minutes, then flip the salmon and begin brushing the glaze over the top. Flip again and continue glazing until the salmon reaches an internal temperature of 120-125°F.

Serve the salmon with the chilled namasu.

Prep time: 15 minutes
Cook time: 45 minutes

**SERVES 4**

# SALT BAKED KANPACHI WITH BUG JUICE

- ½ cup Aloha Shoyu
- ½ cup distilled white vinegar
- 4 tablespoons water
- Juice of 1 lemon
- 1 tablespoon sugar
- 2 teaspoons black pepper
- 3 pounds kosher salt
- ½ cup water
- 2 tablespoons cilantro, minced
- 3 Thai basil leaves, minced
- 3 pound whole kanpachi with scales, gutted (can also use a different fish like branzino or whatever you have)
- Cilantro and Thai basil

*If you only have a larger fish you can leave the head and tail uncovered and just pack the salt mix around the body of the fish.*

*This dish is an absolute joy to make and a true showstopper for your friends or 'ohana. I featured it on my TV show* Eating Our Roots *during the salt episode to highlight the incredible versatility of salt—not just as a seasoning, but as a cooking medium. As I mentioned on the show, you might expect this dish to be overwhelmingly salty given the amount of salt involved, but it's surprisingly balanced. The salt crust locks in moisture, keeping the fish tender and juicy. Since the scales and skin remain intact, the flesh is perfectly protected from over-salting, allowing the natural flavors of the fish to shine through. What makes this dish even more special is the dramatic presentation—revealing the whole fish and cracking open the salt crust tableside is a surefire way to dazzle your guests. Don't let the technique intimidate you; it's simpler than it looks, incredibly rewarding, and a lot of fun. Whether it's the moist, flavorful fish or the unforgettable tableside experience, this dish will leave your guests raving long after the meal.*

---

**Prepare bug juice:** In a bowl, whisk together Aloha Shoyu, vinegar, water, lemon juice, sugar, and pepper. Set aside to allow the flavors to meld.

**Cook fish:** Preheat your oven to 400°F. Line a large baking sheet with foil or parchment paper for easy cleanup.

In a large bowl, combine kosher salt with water until the mixture reaches the texture of moist sand. Stir in the cilantro and basil to infuse the flavors.

Spread a thin, even layer of the salt mixture on the bottom of the baking sheet, creating a base large enough to com-

fortably rest the fish. Place the fish on the salt layer, then cover it completely with the remaining salt mixture, gently pressing it around the fish to fully enclose it. Bake the fish for about 35 minutes, or until the internal temperature reaches 135°F. Remove from the oven and let it rest for 10 minutes to retain moisture.

Crack the salt crust and discard it. Gently peel off the skin, which should come off easily. Using a fish spatula, carefully lift the top fillet off the bones and transfer it to a plate. Repeat for the bottom fillet.

Serve fish with the prepared bug juice as a dipping sauce, garnishing with torn cilantro and Thai basil for a fresh, aromatic finish.

# MISOYAKI BUTTERFISH

**Prep time:** 24 hours (including marinating)
**Cook time:** 20 minutes

**SERVES 6**

1½ cups white miso
1½ cups brown sugar
½ cup mirin
½ cup sake
6 black cod fillets (you can substitute salmon if you can't find black cod)
Pickled ginger for garnish (optional but makes the dish so much better)

*In my early twenties, I had the opportunity to compete on a show called* **The Next Food Network Star.** *It's been so long now that Paula Deen was still a guest judge at the time! For one challenge, we were cooking on a beach in Miami, and while we were allowed to prep the night before, I knew I had to bring my A-game. That's when I decided to pull out my butterfish recipe. Since black cod wasn't available in South Beach, I substituted Chilean sea bass, and it turned out to be a game-changer. The dish was an instant hit! The stakes were high—the winner of the challenge would receive a $20,000 Target gift card, and I knew my wife wouldn't let me come home without it. I put everything into that dish, and it paid off—I won the challenge in spectacular fashion and have been making this recipe ever since. Though simple in its preparation, this dish is packed with layers of umami that make it unforgettable. These days, you'll find it on the menu at most Japanese restaurants, often with a steep price tag. But why not skip the expense and make it at home? It's just as delicious and even more satisfying when you're the one behind the creation.*

---

**Mix marinade:** In a mixing bowl, whisk together miso, sugar, mirin, and sake until smooth and well-combined. Marinate the fish for at least 24 hours to allow the flavors to infuse.

**Cook fish:** When ready to cook, preheat your oven to the high broil setting. Remove the fish from the marinade and place it on a tin foil-lined baking sheet. Position the pan on the middle rack and broil the fish for 8 to 10 minutes. The fish will darken significantly during broiling—this is the caramelization of the sugars, which is key to developing rich flavor.

For balance, I always serve the fish with a side of pickled ginger. The acidity of the ginger cuts through the richness and sweetness of the fish.

# COCONUT SHRIMP

**Prep time:** 1 hour
**Cook time:** 30 minutes

**SERVES 6**

1 large egg
1½ cups all-purpose flour, divided use
½ cup soda water
1½ teaspoons baking powder
2 cups sweetened coconut flakes
25 shrimp, peeled, deveined and butterflied
4 cups neutral oil for frying
1 pineapple, cut into small pieces, discard core
½ can (about 6 ounces) Coco Lopez Cream of Coconut
½ lemon, juiced

*Coconut shrimp has earned its place as a beloved dish worldwide. With the abundance of Kahuku shrimp, Kaua'i shrimp, Kona shrimp, and fresh local coconuts, it's no surprise that Hawaii should produce some of the best coconut shrimp around. This recipe lives up to that promise—one of the best I've ever had. It's everything you want in coconut shrimp: sweet, crispy, and perfectly balanced. While it requires a little time and patience to prepare, I can assure you the result is worth every minute. The combination of juicy, flavorful shrimp and the golden crunch of coconut makes this dish irresistible and well worth the effort.*

**Prepare batter:** In a medium bowl, whisk together the egg, ½ cup of flour, soda water, and baking powder until smooth.

**Prepare shrimp:** In a separate bowl, place the remaining 1 cup of flour. In another bowl, add the coconut flakes.

Hold one shrimp by the tail and dredge it in the flour, shaking off any excess. Dip the floured shrimp into the batter, letting any excess drip off, then roll it in the coconut flakes until evenly coated. Place the coated shrimp on a plate and repeat with the remaining shrimp. Refrigerate for at least 1 hour, or freeze for longer storage.

**Fry shrimp:** In a large pot, heat oil to 350°F. Working in batches, carefully fry the shrimp for 3 to 5 minutes, or until golden brown and fully cooked.

**Make sauce:** In a small pot over medium heat, combine pineapple, coconut cream, and lemon juice. Cook for about 5 minutes, then transfer to a blender. Blend until smooth and thick, resembling a chutney.

*After rolling the shrimp in the coconut flakes, it is very important that you chill them in the refrigerator before cooking. You can even freeze them and cook it straight from frozen. Not only does this help the coconut stick, but it ensures that the shrimp fully cooks before the coconut burns.*

Prep time: 35 minutes
Cook time: 20 minutes

SERVES 4

# FURIKAKE BATTERED SHRIMP TEMPURA

12 large shrimp, peeled and deveined
Neutral oil for frying
1 cup all-purpose flour, sifted, plus 1⁄4 cup for dredging
1 teaspoon salt
1 tablespoon furikake
11⁄4 cup cold soda water with small handful of ice
1 egg beaten
2 cloves black garlic
1⁄4 cup mayonnaise

*This tempura batter is light, crispy, and incredibly easy to make. One of my favorite uses for it is with lobster, but it works just as well with vegetables, other meats, or anything else you'd like to tempura. While tempura batter might seem intimidating at first, following a few simple tips can make all the difference. First, keep the batter cold. Cold batter is key to achieving that perfect crispiness. If you're making a large batch, place your mixing bowl over ice to help maintain the chill, which is why we add ice directly to the batter. Second, make sure to dredge all your ingredients first. For vegetables, I dip them in water before dredging them in flour—this helps the flour stick. Then, dip them into the cold batter, which ensures the batter clings on properly and doesn't slide off during frying. Lastly, always use clean oil. Tempura absorbs the flavor of the oil, so if the oil is dirty, it will affect the taste of your food. By following these simple steps, I promise you'll impress your family and guests with your tempura skills.*

**Prepare shrimp:** Starting from the tail, slice the shrimp in half lengthwise, stopping at the head to butterfly them open (see photo, left, for reference).

In a large pot, heat oil to 350°F for frying.

**Prep tempura batter:** In a bowl, sift 1 cup of all-purpose flour, then add salt and furikake seasoning. Mix to combine.

In a measuring cup, add a small handful of ice and fill with soda water until you reach a total of 11⁄4 cups.

**Make tempura batter:** Add the egg to the flour mixture, then pour in the iced soda water. Gently mix with a fork or

chopsticks. Be careful not to overmix—lumps in the batter are fine.

**Dredge shrimp:** In a separate bowl, place ¼ cup of flour for dredging. Hold the shrimp by the tail and dredge it in the flour, shaking off any excess. Dip the shrimp into the tempura batter, letting any excess drip off. A thin coating of batter will create a light, crispy texture.

**Fry shrimp:** Carefully add the shrimp to the hot oil and fry for about 5 minutes, or until golden and crispy.

**Make sauce:** Mash the black garlic into a paste and mix it well with mayonnaise to create the sauce.

*If you are doing a big batch of shrimp or vegetables, you can par cook most of it and right before serving, drop it back into hot oil and finish it to a crispy golden brown.*

# IPPY'S PANTRY ESSENTIALS

My pantry is like a living organism, changing and adapting based on its current environment. What I am currently into, what I have discovered, and what I have been doing all affect it. However, there are essentials that I couldn't live without. Whenever I do competitions on the Food Network or other stations, they usually give us the opportunity to bring a handful of ingredients. That is when I break into my pantry and start pondering what exactly I use most. The following will give you a great foundation for what you need for the recipes in this book, and to just have a well-stocked pantry to help you through whatever culinary endeavor that is thrown your way.

**Aloha Shoyu**—Soy sauce is king in Hawaiian food. We use it not only to season our rice, but we use it in most of our sauces as well. The fermented salty umami bomb is truly an essential ingredient. If I had to pick only one brand to use for the rest of my life, the decision is simple. Aloha Shoyu is the best. The flavor is distinct yet doesn't overpower whatever you are making.

**Apple cider vinegar or rice vinegar**—In Hawai'i, we have a large Filipino community and their tastes are reflected in our dishes. This is the key ingredient in not only my adobo, but also in orange sauce, lemon sauce, tinono, and so much more. Apple cider has a sweeter taste, but

rice vinegar is my favorite as its subtle and can be incorporated into so many dishes.

**Chili Crunch**—Chili crunch has made a big statement in recent years. Growing up, I always saw chili oil at most of my favorite restaurants. Chili crunch takes chili oil to a whole new level! I have a delicious recipe in this book (page 35). I promise you that making a batch of this and keeping it on hand will be one of the best decisions you make.

**Furikake**—This ingredient is something that is also found in every local family's pantry. Furikake is a mixture of all things umami, toasted sesame, and roasted nori mixed together with salt. Most uses involve dusting your rice with this. At the restaurant, we put it in all our bento boxes. It is also used for crusting fish, specifically ʻahi, before lightly searing it. Furikake is a must.

**Garlic powder**—You probably already have this ingredient in your pantry, but in case you don't here is your sign.

**Hawaiian salt**—Hawaiian salt to me is unmatched. If you can't find Hawaiian sea salt, coarse sea salt will also do. The objective is to have salt that doesn't just melt the second it hits the meat. It is crucial and the sole ingredient in kālua pig and the secret to my prime rib crust. Hawaiian salt has a major problem as many companies try to say their salt is Hawaiian salt when it really isn't. Regulations have not yet been put in place to stop this.

**Miso**—Growing up, we always had instant miso packs in the house for a quick snack. In my house, I always have miso paste on hand. When it comes to the type of miso, white miso is my favorite. I use it for misoyaki, miso glaze, miso risotto, and for a simple miso soup. You can

use red miso in a pinch, just know it will have a bit of a more pungent taste.

**MSG**—Monosodium glutamate is a controversial ingredient as some people can be very sensitive to this ingredient. A little goes a long way, and when you are eating a dish with it and realize there is something in there you can't quite pick out but also can't stop eating, it is probably msg. This ingredient is probably in your favorite snack from potato chips to soup. MSG is an umami powerhouse when used correctly.

**Patis**—Fish sauce! Yes, I know it might not be the best smelling, but it is definitely one of the best tasting things that adds an extra kick to anything. Usually made with anchovies, which are not only one of my favorite ingredients, I also have them tattooed on my arm. I can't live without their salty umami-packed deliciousness.

**Rice**—When it comes to Hawaiian plate lunch, nothing is complete without a scoop (or two) of white rice. Specifically, short grain rice, and the preferred brand in Hawai'i is Calrose. The rice has to be sticky and form into a ball that can be scooped or molded. This ingredient can't be left out. Whenever a Hawaiian is far from home, nine times out of ten they will say that what they miss most is their rice! For breakfast, lunch, and dinner, this sticky starchy ingredient is definitely essential.

# INDEX

## D



## E

## H



## I



## J



## K



## L

## M



## N



## O

## P

## R



## S

## T



## U



## V

# PHOTO CREDITS

All photos by Dustin Acdal
unless otherwise noted below.

Photos courtesy Ippy Aiona
  Pages vii (top), xx (bottom), xxi, xxiii (all), xxiv (top), 2 (top), 3 (bottom right), 6, 27, 39 (bottom left and right), 40 (bottom), 59, 78, 79 (all), 80 (all), 84, 118, 120 (top), 176 (top and center)

Photos courtesy of Aria Studios, from *Eating Our Roots* episodes 1-8
  Pages ii (all), vi (all except for top left), vii (bottom), ix (center), xi (center and bottom), xiv (all except for top right), xvi, 2 (bottom), 3 (top left), 9, 11, 13 (all), 14, 18, 22, 30, 38, 42, 46, 58, 64, 65 (all), 72, 76, 82, 85, 90, 91, 93, 94, 95 (all), 102, 103, 107 (left, top and bottom), 110, 115, 116, 121, 122, 129, 132, 133, 141, 143, 148, 149, 153, 154 (all), 155 (all), 176 (bottom)

Photos from dreamstime.com
  Pages iii, vi (top left), ix (bottom), x (bottom), xi (top), xv, xvii, xix, xx (top), 1, 7, 29, 34, 36, 37, 41, 47, 48, 49, 66, 67, 77, 81, 83, 99, 108, 114, 117, 119 (all), 127, 142, 147,– 158, 163 (center and bottom), 164 (all)

Photo by Candes Gentry, courtesy of Aloha Green, page 17

Photo by Tom Takada, page 174

*« Photographer Dustin Acdal.*

# ABOUT THE AUTHOR

Chef Ippy Aiona was born and raised on the Big Island of Hawai'i, where his passion for food was shaped by his family. His father ran a Hawaiian plate lunch shop, and his mother owned an Italian restaurant, giving him an early appreciation for both cuisines. Building on this, he opened several successful restaurant concepts on the Big Island, including Ippy's Hawaiian BBQ, The Dizzy Pita, and the gastropub The Three Fat Pigs.

Chef Ippy's rise in the culinary world has been impressive. After graduating at the top of his class from Le Cordon Bleu in San Francisco, he quickly made a name for himself. At just twenty-three, he became the youngest finalist on Food Network's *Next Food Network Star,* gaining national attention. His charisma and skill earned him regular appearances on Food Network, including shows like *BBQ Brawl, Alex vs America,* and his own locally produced television series, *Eating Our Roots,* currently available on KHNL's *Hawaii News Now.*

*Eating Our Roots* is a culinary travel series that Chef Ippy wrote, co-produced, and hosted. The show explores the cultural heritage behind local cuisines, celebrating ancestral food traditions while connecting with communities and showcasing the ingredients and flavors that shape regional identity.

At age twenty-four, Chef Ippy earned a spot on *Forbes'* "30 Under 30" list, recognizing his creativity and contributions to the food industry. He also won Canada's prestigious International Iron Chef competition, further showcasing his culinary expertise.

In April 2022, Chef Ippy released his first cookbook, *Easy Hawaiian Cookbook: 70 Simple Recipes for a Taste of the Islands,* which reached Amazon's top 100 cookbooks. His culinary approach reflects the unique blend of his Hawaiian roots and Italian heritage, resulting in a style that continues to draw attention. Chef Ippy's journey is a testament to his dedication, creativity, and love for sharing the flavors of his culture.

Chef Ippy
Chef Ippy